The Playwright as Magician

The Playwright as Magician

Shakespeare's Image of the Poet
in the
English Public Theater

ALVIN B. KERNAN

NEW HAVEN AND LONDON
YALE UNIVERSITY PRESS
1979

Published with assistance from
the Louis Effingham deForest Memorial Fund.

Designed by Christopher Harris
and set in Aster type.
Printed in the United States of America by
The Vail-Ballou Press, Binghamton, N.Y.

Published in Great Britain, Europe, Africa, and
Asia (except Japan) by Yale University Press,
Ltd., London. Distributed in Australia and
New Zealand by Book & Film Services, Artarmon,
N.S.W., Australia; and in Japan by Harper & Row,
Publishers, Tokyo Office.

Library of Congress Cataloging in Publication Data

Kernan, Alvin B
    The playwright as magician.

Includes index.
    1. Shakespeare, William, 1564–1616—Criticism and
interpretation.2. Theater—England—History.
I. Title.
PR2976.K48   822.3'3   79–10829
ISBN 0–300–02379–0

Contents

Acknowledgments

Although the present book is primarily new material, it contains the bones of several earlier articles, extensively revised and rearranged: "This Goodly Frame, the Stage," *Shakespeare Quarterly;* "Shakespeare's Essays on Dramatic Poesy," Yale University Press; "Formalism and Realism in Elizabethan Drama," *Renaissance Drama;* "Shakespeare and the Abstraction of History," the University of Delaware Press; and an essay on *Hamlet* from *Character and Conflict,* Harcourt, Brace, Jovanovich. I am grateful to the original publishers for permission to reprint this material. I would also like to express my gratitude to the Andrew W. Mellon Foundation for the chair and the academic arrangements which made possible the completion of this book.

1

The Poet's Place in the World
Images of the Poet
in the
Renaissance

The conception of poetry in a given age is always focused and set by some particularly striking image of the poet, which becomes the model for the other poets who live and write in that tradition. This dominant image of the poet, which may be established as a character in literature or be personified in the life of a particular poet—usually both—contains in itself a theory of both the nature of the true poet and the sources, forms, and functions of poetry. Milton's image of himself in *Paradise Lost* and in his life—blind, isolated, "fall'n on evil days"—expresses a conception of poetry as inward, divinely inspired, and addressing "fit audience though few." In later times Wordsworth was to create another dominant image of the poet as a solitary dweller in nature, seeking in his mind and memories the guarantee of his own poetic genius; and in a still later time Joyce's Stephen Dedalus, exiled, wandering, seeking a father, trying to forge in the smithy of his soul the uncreated conscience of his race, gave another age of writers their image of the poet and fixed their definition of poetry.

Although one particular image of the poet tends to dominate at a given time, once a powerful and effective image has been created, it tends to remain in play for a long time, affecting subsequent images and offering alternative models to the poets who come after.

Modern literature may be said to have begun when Francis Petrarch (1304–74) created an image of the poet which dominated the early Renaissance and which has profoundly influenced all subsequent images of the poet and definitions of poetry. There were, of course, many writers of poetry before Petrarch, but insofar as he was, as has often been said, the first modern man, so was he also in many ways the first modern poet, the first writer to conceive in a modern way of the existence and importance of a particular kind of writing we now call literature. Although Petrarch says of himself that he "should not wish to appear to be a poet and nothing more,"[1] his modernity appears nowhere more clearly than in his professionalism, his continuous self-conscious awareness of himself as a poet and writer above all things else. His writings were preoccupied with poetry, and his own life was a carefully constructed enactment of a role which defined the essential qualities of the poet and poetry for his time.

Petrarch fixed his image of the poet and of poetry in a most remarkable fashion in the coronation with laurels which he designed for himself and staged on April 8, Easter Sunday, 1341, in the Senate House on the Capitoline Hill in Rome. Medieval anonymity was here cast aside as the poet took up a heroic stance as an individual and claimed a new social importance for the poet and his art. Petrarch was anxious to support his poetic image and his views of poetry with the full weight of tradition, and so he claimed that in his coronation he was merely reinstituting an ancient Roman ceremony of crowning the poet with laurels. But while there

1. "Petrarch's Coronation Oration," ed. and trans. Ernest Hatch Wilkins, *Studies in the Life and Works of Petrarch* (Cambridge, Mass.: Medieval Academy of America, 1955), p. 307.

had been a few ancient and contemporary coronations, it had certainly never been a traditional ritual, and certainly the high claims that Petrarch made for poetry had never before been given such full ceremonial statement.

Offers of the laurel, clearly solicited in the first instance by Petrarch, were made to him on the same day, September 1, 1340, by the Roman Senate and by the University of Paris. Petrarch chose Rome over Paris—chose that is, the classical tradition for which he was such a prominent spokesman all his life, over the medieval scholastic tradition represented by the University of Paris. But the shift to the classical model was by no means complete and many medieval elements remained in the ceremony. The oration delivered during the ceremony was structured like a medieval sermon, and Petrarch arranged to have his worthiness of the laurels tested in an oral examination on poetry, history, and philosophy, something like that given by medievel universities for a doctor's degree, administered by King Robert of Naples and Sicily, a powerful ruler with a reputation for learning and wisdom who had been influential in arranging the offer of the laurels. Petrarch was duly certified by King Robert as having passed the examination; and thus licensed to practice poetry, he journeyed to Rome for his coronation, arriving on April 6th, Good Friday, 1341. On Easter Sunday, April 8, the coronation took place:

> a procession was formed, headed by twelve noble youths in scarlet, reciting poems composed by Petrarch for the occasion. Then came six principal citizens, in green and crowned with flowers. Then the Senator, Orso dell'Anguillara, Petrarch's host at Capranica in 1337. He wore a laurel wreath, as did his eminent attendants, among them old Stefano Colonna. The procession climbed the Capitoline Hill, the site of the Temple of Jupiter. It entered the twelfth-century Senatorial Palace and mounted to the audience chamber on the second floor.

The officials took their places. Trumpets sounded, and the candidate for the laureateship was bidden to stand forth. He appeared, bareheaded, wearing King Robert's royal gown. He pronounced his Coronation Oration, lasting about half an hour, and concluded with a request for the laurel crown of poetry. He then cried three times: "Long live the Roman people and the Senator, and God maintain them in liberty!" He knelt before the Senator, who after a short speech asked the assembled citizens if they approved the award. They did so, weeping. The Senator took from his head the laurel crown and placed it on Petrarch's, saying: "This crown is the reward of merit." Petrarch recited a sonnet on the heroes of Rome, which has not survived. The audience clapped and shouted: "Long live the Capitol and the Poet!" Petrarch admits that he was in a kind of intoxication, blushing at the applause and praise.[2]

It should be noted that while the Senatorial Palace on the Capitoline had been in fact built in the middle of the twelfth century, Petrarch believed it to be the original building in which Cicero, the Roman writer he most admired and whose works he collected and edited, had actually spoken.

Recent Petrarch criticism has begun to teach us some of the subtle ways by which the poet encoded his symbolic meanings in his poetry, and the coronation and its interior oration seem to have been as carefully structured in this regard as his poems. His entrance into Rome, for example, was on the sixth of April, and that date carried many meanings for Petrarch,

2. Morris Bishop, *Petrarch and His World* (Bloomington: Indiana University Press, 1963), p. 168. The most careful and detailed study of the ceremony is Ernest Hatch Wilkins, "The Coronation of Petrarch," in *The Making of the Canzoniere and Other Petrarchan Studies* (Rome: *Edizione di storia e letteratura*, 1951), pp. 9–69. Petrarch himself describes the coronation in his *Familiar Letters*, IV. 4.

on the sixth day man was created and on sixth he fell, and on the sixth [the traditional "absolute" date for Good Friday] Christ's death redeemed that fall. Petrarch would have us believe that this same sixth of April was equally important in his life: on the sixth of April 1327 he first saw Laura; on the sixth of April 1338 he first was inspired to write the *Africa;* on the sixth of April 1348 Laura died.[3]

The laurel with which Petrarch was crowned carried an equally heavy symbolic meaning, containing in itself not only its traditional values of fame and the permanence of evergreens, but referring as well to his beloved Laura, to the disdainful Daphne who was turned by Apollo the god of poetry into a laurel tree, and, in Christological interpretations, to the cross on which Christ was crucified.[4]

If the modern reader fails to perceive some of these more arcane meanings, it still remains startlingly obvious that the coronation was designed to present the poet in the role of Christ. The entry into Rome on Good Friday parallels the beginning of the Passion, as well as the earlier entry into Jerusalem, and the coronation on Easter Sunday, the Resurrection. But in the coronation ceremony poetic values are substituted for the traditional religious concepts. In the oration delivered as the central piece of the coronation, Petrarch notes Cicero's remark that "Ennius fairly calls poets sacred in their own right," and speaks of "a certain inner and divinely given energy . . . infused in the poet's spirit,"[5] thus making poetic inspiration the artistic equivalent of Christ's divine nature and God-given mission.

---

3. Thomas P. Roche, Jr., "The Calendrical Structure of Petrarch's *Canzoniere,*" *Studies in Philology* 71 (1974): 163–64.

4. See Thomas P. Roche, Jr., "Ovid's Daphne, Petrarch's *Canzoniere,* and their Sixteenth Century Commentators," forthcoming book.

5. "Petrarch's Coronation Oration," p. 301. Subsequent quotes from the oration are identified in the text by page numbers in Wilkins's translation.

Classical literary texts—those of Vergil, Juvenal, Cicero, Ovid, Horace—which Petrarch so admired and knowledge of which he helped to spread so widely, become in the oration his sacred texts, and he quotes them frequently and as exactly as his knowledge allowed, with the care befitting words bearing such important meanings as he attributes to them. The key text is taken not from the Bible but from Vergil's *Georgics*, "But a sweet longing urges me upward over the lonely slopes of Parnassus"; and Parnassus becomes the poet's Calvary as Petrarch goes on to detail the painful difficulty of the poet's task, the "bitterness of fortune" which impedes the paths of all poets, including himself, and the failure of the world to appreciate poets and poetry. There had been once a poetic Eden,

> an age that was happier for poets, an age when they were held in the highest honor, first in Greece and then in Italy, and especially when Caesar Augustus held imperial sway, under whom there flourished excellent poets, Virgil, Varus [*sic.,*] Ovid, Horace, and many others.[303]

It is this golden age of poetry that the poet through love—*per ardua dulcis / raptat amor*[6]—suffering, and labors is bringing back in his revival of the coronation with laurel and the revivification of poetry in his own writings which the ceremony celebrates.

But there were presences other than Christ on the Capitoline that Easter morning. The laurel crown, Petrarch argues, was in ancient times "the due reward of Caesars and of poets," and Petrarch the great classicist identifies himself and his poetry with "the memory of [Rome's] great men: 'twas here they dwelt, 'twas here they sat, 'twas here they engaged in their philosophical discussions.'"[7] By standing in

6. *Georgics*, III, 291–92.
7. "Petrarch's Coronation Oration," p. 305. Petrarch is quoting Plato, *Laws* II.2.

6

the place where they had stood, the poet in his secular aspect becomes the image of Caesar, striving by means of his inspiration and his poetic skill to restore honor to Rome and to Italy, to achieve personal glory for himself, and to encourage others to "like endeavor." The poet is not, in Petrarch's view, a mere inventor of fictions, but the possessor of "a certain genius given. . .from on high"(306), driven by an "intense longing" to set forth "in the stable and enduring style of a true man of letters"(308) "under the veil of fictions. . .truths physical, moral, and historical. . ."(307). Poetry will guarantee fame to the state and to its great men, and will preserve the name of the poet for posterity. The laurel, Petrarch concludes, is the fitting symbol of these secular powers of poetry: its fragrance signifies poetry's good repute; its leaves are incorruptible and thus signify the eternity of poetic fame; it is sacred to Apollo and so are Caesars and poets; it is appropriate to poets in that it makes dreams come true and "promises foreknowledge of the future"; and it is immune to lightning, the image of the destructive powers of time.

To appreciate the full power of the secular claims Petrarch was making for the poet in joining him with Caesar and with the glory of the Roman past evoked by that name, it is necessary to remember that the greatness of the city was, in 1341, only an idea in the mind of an inspired classicist like Petrarch. The actual city lay in piles of rubble and broken forms below the Capitoline, the population had shrunk to below 50,000 people, the pope had moved the seat of Christianity to Avignon, the streets were the battleground of rival gangs of nobles, and the approaches were controlled by groups of bandits. In figuring the poet as the Caesar who would restore Rome to its former glory, Petrarch was claiming as much for his art as he was in conceiving him as a Christ figure who through his suffering and lonely toil would save man and restore him to the Edenic state.

Immediately after the coronation, the procession went to St. Peter's, and there, like some medieval poet writing his

palinode, Petrarch laid his laurel crown on the altar. To us,
looking back from the twentieth century, his submission to
the church inevitably seems a diminishing of the high boasts,
made at the coronation, that the poet had now become a
Christ and Caesar, the savior of the city of God and the city
of man. This, after all, was to be the role that poets claimed
in the modern world as belief in Christ and Caesar waned,
and so any submission to them seems a surrender of the
primacy of art to a church and state which used art merely
as a means to a higher end.

Such a view of the powers of the poet may have been
historically inevitable, but Petrarch would no doubt have
been troubled by it. He, after all, lived out his life supported
by appointments in the church, having taken minor orders,
and religious belief was a deep and permanent part of his
personal life. For him, Christ was the image of the fully lived
Christian life, and thus to cast the poet in the image of Christ
was not to replace Christ with the poet, religion with art, but
only to imitate the ideal. Both Christ and Caesar were
models or parallels, similar to but existing on separate levels
from the poet. To lay the poetic laurels on the altar was only
to affirm the true hierarchy of things, a hierarchy that was
probably never really forgotten in the coronation.

We know that the difference between the poet and
Caesar, and the ultimate dependence of the first on the
second, were not finally blurred in Petrarch's mind, for in
his epic poem the *Africa*, the poet Ennius is made a follower
and close friend of the hero Scipio Africanus. Ennius
instructs Scipio, on his triumphant return voyage from
Africa, that true poetry is not mere amusement but a fiction
based on truth which preserves the hero's glory, insures his
eternal fame, and provides moral examples for ages to come.
Ennius also relates a dream in which Homer appeared to
him and, after foretelling the future greatness of Ennius as
"another Homer," predicted that in Italy in the distant
future there would be another great poet, *Francisco cui nomen
erit* (IX.233). Upon their return to Rome, Scipio and Ennius

climb the Capitoline to be crowned together: "the central image is that of the sacred poet, from Homer through Ennius to Petrarch, seeking to play his ordained role as dispenser of truth and glory, but enjoying proper recognition only under enlightened monarchs."[8]

But as Petrarch says in his oration, "when a person who is asleep is touched with laurel his dreams come true,"(311) and just as Ennius's dream came true, by Petrarch's artistic contrivance of making his *Africa* the realization of the dream it contained, so did the dream of the poet and poetry which Petrarch created on the Capitoline eventually become a reality. In time the world accepted Petrarch's conceptions of the poet as being another Christ and Caesar, of the classical literary and poetic texts as sacred books, of poetry as the guardian of the moral health of nations, and of the ability of poetry to confer the laurel's immortality on the works of men and protect them against the ravages of time. Petrarch created on the Capitoline a heroic image of the poet as the savior of men's souls and the guardian of the welfare of nations which dominated the Renaissance and has, in the various derivative forms created by such poets as Milton and Wordsworth, lasted on into and deeply influenced the present.

Nearly two hundred years later in an Italian court a new image of the poet appeared which, while not obliterating the Petrarchan model, offered a competing conception to the imagination of another generation of poets in the late Renaissance. The new poet was not a single heroic figure like Petrarch striving to redeem a fallen world, but a courtly amateur, moving easily and gracefully in Castiglione's *Courtier*, published in 1528, among a group of fashionable ladies and gentlemen at the court of Urbino, speaking wittily and gracefully about poetry as a necessary accomplishment of the gentleman. The Petrarchan inspired genius and dedi-

---

8. Aldo S. Bernardo, *Petrarch, Scipio and the "Africa," The Birth of Humanism's Dream* (Baltimore: The Johns Hopkins Press, 1962), p. 162.

cated professional poet with a heroic mission are replaced here by the accomplished amateur, by a poet for whom poetry is only a part of a life lived fully in society, as the setting indicates, communicating with other men and women of similar aristocratic tastes, helping to create a good and gracious way of life by manifesting in language the refined manners and morals valued by the court. Petrarch and Boccaccio are mentioned frequently and reverently by these lords and ladies of Urbino, but the professional zeal of those older poets has disappeared from the courtly conception of poetry.

Instead, the concern for language and style of the Petrarchan tradition is emphasized, and poetry is treated as a form of speaking well, of elegant and effective conversation, but one manifestation of a courtly way of life, and but one activity of the gentleman-scholar-courtier. At Urbino, true poetry expresses in linguistic terms the elegant, graceful ways of living, and the high ideals, which also find expression in other forms of civilized life such as dance, dress, manners, love, and courtly service. As Daniel Javitch puts it, speaking of the relation of courtly poetry and courtly life in Tudor England, the artifices of poetry were esteemed because of "their resemblance to the artifices courtiers themselves sought to display in their conduct. . . .because the distinctive features of poetry were so congenial to courtly habits of mind and style, poets or their supporters could accord the art a more important social function than it had been granted."[9]

9. *Poetry and Courtliness in Renaissance England* (Princeton, N.J.: Princeton University Press, 1978), p. 6. This fine book establishes in detail the way in which the type of poetry defined in *The Courtier* became the dominant conception of poetry in Tudor England, and argues with great skill that it became dominant because it fitted certain social views and needs of the time. Javitch provides a perfect case study of the more general argument that the motive force behind the conception of poetry at any given time is not some universal aesthetic impulse but rather the need to find a way to make concrete and to validate a particular set of social values.

Each detail in the personality of the courtly poet and each characteristic of the courtly poetic style reflect directly courtly values and manners. Since the courtier does not seek money or vulgar reputation, the courtly poet does not publish his poetry but contents himself with circulation of his writings among his own circle. The poet is expected, of course, to write in moral ways about suitably aristocratic subjects, but the actual content of poetry is of less interest to the court at Urbino than is style, for values are conveyed in poetry, as elsewhere, through doing the right things in the appropriate way. Poetry must, like life, strive toward the beautiful, which is to say it must be mellifluous, sweet, harmonious, tempered, and seemly. It must not be labored, no matter what labor has gone into it, but polished and easy in manner, conveying the all-important quality of *sprezzatura*, that graceful way of doing difficult things with an appearance of ease, without earnestness or show of pedantic labor. Avoiding turgidity and difficulty always, poetry should "express well and clearly what the mind conceives," being clear, precise, and having a "lucid fullness." Nor should it be too sparse, but should be, rather, "universal, copious, varied," and should, finally, through "facility, good order, fullness, fine periods and harmonious clauses," stir up the appropriate sentiments in the minds of its listeners. It should not be heavily dogmatic or tendentious, but should display that "flexible capacity to embody opposites, the difficult moderation that Castiglione calls *mediocrità*,[10] a mixture of gravity and levity, wit and seriousness, clarity and elaboration, open to and combining a variety of points of view. The emphasis on style, on language, on communication and social life conveys in *The Courtier* a most noble and elevated, entirely humane conception of the poet as a man fully sensitive to and fully skilled in that most human of activities, language, and fully participating in the life of his society to further the courtly virtues

10. *Ibid.*, p. 31.

of skill, grace, clarity, balance, harmony, and "simplicity and nonchalance."[11]

Looking back from the present, Shakespeare and Jonson, Spenser and Donne, appear the great English poetic figures of their time, but in the 1590s the ideal and model for all other poets was Sir Philip Sidney (1554–86), who established and lived out, in England, the role of the courtly poet depicted in *The Courtier*. Poetry was for Sidney, as for Castiglione's courtier, only a part, though a closely integrated and important part, of a much larger social life of learning, travel abroad, service leading to a place at court, foreign embassies, involvement in religious and political causes, a brilliant marriage, a fashionably hopeless love affair with Stella (Penelope Rich), martial adventure, overseas exploration, and finally a glorious and exemplary death from a battle wound in the Lowlands' wars, received because of his chivalric gallantry in refusing to wear armor that another lacked. Ophelia's description of Hamlet as he once had been very much catches the spirit of the perfect courtier and universal man Sidney was for his times:

The courtier's, soldier's, scholar's eye, tongue, sword,
Th' expectancy and rose of the fair state,
The glass of fashion, and the mold of form,
Th' observed of all observers. . . .

[3.1.152–55][12]

And indeed it is in terms very close to Ophelia's that Sidney's close friend and relative, Fulke-Greville, described him about 1595:

---

11. The most important sections on poetry in *The Courtier* are I, 29–53. Quotations used here are from the translation of Charles Singleton (New York: Anchor Books, 1959).

12. All Shakespeare citations are from *The Complete Signet Classic Shakespeare*, gen. ed. Sylvan Barnet (New York: Harcourt Brace Jovanovich, 1972.)

Indeed he was a true modell of Worth; A man fit for Conquest, Plantation, Reformation, or what Action soever is greatest, and hardest amongst men. . . . The Universities abroad, and at home, accompted him a generall *Maecenas* of Learning; Dedicated their Books to him; and communicated every Invention, or Improvement of Knowledge with him. Souldiers honoured him, and were so honoured by him, as no man thought he marched under the true Banner of *Mars*, that had not obtained Sir *Philip Sidney's* approbation. Men of Affairs in most parts of Christendome, entertained correspondency with him. . . .there was not a cunning Painter, a skilfull Engenier, an excellent Musician, or any other Artificer of extraordinary fame, that made not himself known to this famous Spirit and found him his true friend without hire. . . .[13]

Sidney's understanding of the nature and function of poetry, as expressed primarily in the *Apology for Poetry*, was as humane as the role he lived out, but his conception of the poet included something of the Petrarchan heroic ideal as well as of the courtly poet of Castiglione. To Sidney it seemed perfectly natural that Alexander could have carried a copy of Homer with him on his conquests, for the great poets were for him true seers and the revealers of profound truths, as well as men of practical affairs. He begins the *Apology* by offering a Petrarchan conception of the poet as the first thinker and bringer of light in all societies, antedating both the philosopher and historian. Orpheus, David, Homer, Dante, and Chaucer are "makers," who do not merely imitate nature but create purely imaginary worlds which give substance to the ideal. In his famous phrasing,

13. *Sir Fulke Greville's Life of Sir Philip Sidney* (written ca. 1595, first published 1652), ed. Nowell Smith (Oxford: Clarendon Press, 1907) pp. 33–34.

> Nature never set forth the earth in so rich tapistry as divers Poets have done, neither with plesant rivers, fruitful trees, sweet smelling flowers, nor whatsoever els may make the too much loved earth more lovely. Her world is brasen, the Poets only deliver a golden.[14]

But then he concludes realistically that "these arguments wil by fewe be understood, and by fewer granted,"[15] and goes on to define the poet in a less mystical fashion as someone who feigns "notable images of vertues, vices, or what els"[16] in order to teach and delight. Sidney's true poet never imitates the world exactly—only the meanest poets do this—but rather shows us "what may and should be" by combining the specifics of history with the abstractions of philosophy to present images of virtue and vice vividly and directly. Ajax is the defining image of anger, Agamemnon of pride, and Chaucer's Pandarus of greed.

Sidney's conception of poetry was as wide as it was humane, and while his literary training was primarily in the classics, he was interested in the Irish satirists who rhymed rats to death, and was greatly moved by the border songs of Percy and Douglas. When on an embassy abroad he heard the Hungarians singing "songes of their Auncestours valour" he was able to associate these national epics with Pindar's celebration of victories and the songs that the Lacedaemonians sang at home and in the field. He believed that the Bible is poetry and that David and the prophets were poets who wrote sacred verse not unrelated to various kinds of secular writing. Since he did not believe that meter and rhyme are necessary to poetry, he allowed prose within the category of literary art. English poetry was important to him, and he knew and praised the work of his English predecessors and encouraged the work of his contemporaries.

14. *Apology for Poetry*, in *Elizabethan Critical Essays*, ed. G. Gregory Smith (Oxford: Clarendon Press, 1904), 1: 156.
15. *Ibid.*, p. 157.
16. *Ibid.*, p. 160.

Sidney's broad and humane conception of the nature and function of literature was primarily courtly in spirit, while modified by Petrarchan idealism and English moral practicality, and it was equally courtly in being based on a belief in the value of the rules which should govern and order artistic making. He knew the models of classical literature thoroughly and shared the values which his tradition derived from them: a seemly style, the maintenance of decorum, and the importance of the neo-Aristotelean unities of place, time, and action. He understood metrical theory and had a good historical command of metrics; he was sensitive to the proper and controlled use of tropes such as allegory and various kinds of figurative speech; and he knew the major genres—lyric, tragedy, heroic poem, comedy, elegiac, pastoral—and defined their conventions and purposes. In Sidney we encounter for the first time in English a systematic theory of poetry, and that theory agrees with its courtly origin in firmly grounding poetry on knowledge and art which control and order the imagination of the poet.

In his lifetime Sidney published none of his major writings—neither the prose romance *Arcadia*, the sonnet sequence *Astrophel and Stella*, nor his poetics, the *Apology for Poetry*—and he himself tells us that "as I never desired the title [of poet], so have I neglected the meanes to come by it."[17] The courtly tradition in which he lived and wrote required him to scorn the kinds of writers who "think it inough if they can be rewarded of the Printer,"[18] and his aristocratic connections and position in society, however

17. *Ibid.*, p. 195.
18. *Ibid.*, p. 194. For a survey of the courtly attitude toward print, see J.W. Saunders, "The Stigma of Print, A Note on the Social Bases of Tudor Poetry," *Essays in Criticism* 1 (1951): 139–64. There is even some evidence that manuscripts were still considered by some intellectuals and collectors at this late date to be superior to the printed book. This attitude is a holdover from the earliest days of printing when efforts were made to print books to look like manuscripts, and some collectors would not admit printed works to their libraries.

precarious, enabled him to live out the ideal role of the courtly poet:

> his end was not writing, even while he wrote; nor his knowledge moulded for tables, or schooles; but both his wit, and understanding bent upon his heart, to make himself and others, not in words or opinion, but in life, and action, good and great.[19]

Ben Jonson's remark that "Sidney was no pleasant man in Countenance, his face being spoilled with Pimples,"[20] reminds us of the grim actualities of Sidney's life, but also, since Jonson in his remarks to Drummond was debunking his chief rivals, suggests the extent to which Sidney had become the ideal poet in his time. In him, as John Danby says, "Poetry and learning are for the purposes of realizing a life rather than obtaining a living,"[21] and for him poetry could therefore be "equally above the need for patronage or the necessity to publish."[22]

But poetry is not an absolute and unchanging mode of writing, and the image of the poet and his poetry changes in response to major changes in social and intellectual conditions of the kind that were taking place in the late Elizabethan period. Various changes in the circumstances affecting the writer which we now take for granted—the shift to professionalism, the necessity of seeking patronage from the court and the new Tudor aristocracy, the growing importance of printing, the opening up of a free marketplace in which art could be sold as a commodity, and the appearance of a public and popular art in the theater—were nothing less

---

19. *Fulke Greville's Life,* p. 18.
20. *Conversations With Drummond,* lines 230–31, in *Ben Jonson,* ed. C.H. Herford and Percy and Evelyn Simpson (Oxford: Clarendon Press, 1925–52), 1: 138–39.
21. John Danby, *Elizabethan and Jacobean Poets,* originally published as *Poets on Fortune's Hill* (London: Methuen, 1952), p. 33.
22. *Ibid.,* pp. 32–33.

than revolutionary in their eventual effects upon the conception of literary art.

Before the middle of the sixteenth century there had not been very many English poets, and almost all of them had been amateurs, in the sense that poetry was not their primary occupation or means of earning a living. But in the latter half of the century, a considerable number of young men, largely from the middle and lower-middle classes, trained in the new humanistic education with its literary orientation and encouraged by the new market for literature created by the increase of printing and literacy, began to think of poetry and writing in general as a way of life. For these writers the image of what a poet was and did was ideally the role established by *The Courtier*, echoed in such later works as Puttenham's *Arte of English Poesie*, and embodied in Sidney. But most of the new writers, William Shakespeare among them, lacked the social position and the economic means to treat poetry as a way "of realizing a life rather than obtaining a living." Instead, they were forced to become professional poets and to seek their livings from patronage or from the public by writing for the printer or for the new public theaters.[23] The conflict thus set up between the ideal of who and what the poet was and the actual conditions in which the new poets lived and wrote would eventually be resolved by the creation of a new image of the poet, and it is the purpose of this book to trace the way in which that new image was gradually worked out in the writings of William Shakespeare. But the first reaction of the new poets to their inability to live out the role of the true courtly poet in the circumstances in which they had to write was one of disorientation and agonized confusion. John Donne, who adhered throughout his life to the courtly tradition in his refusal to publish his poems or write for

23. For a complete discussion of the practical difficulties professional poets of the time faced, see E.H. Miller, *The Professional Writer in Elizabethan England, A Study of Nondramatic Literature* (Cambridge, Mass.: Harvard University Press, 1959).

money, expresses most powerfully the new poet's lack of an established identity and a place in the world:

> I would fain do something, but that I cannot tell what is no wonder. For to choose is to do; but to be no part of any body is to be nothing. At most, the greatest persons are but great wens and excrescences; men of wit and delightful conversation but as moles for ornament, except they be so incorporated into the body of the world that they contribute something to the sustentation of the whole.
>
> This I made account that I begun early, when I understood the study of our laws; but was diverted by the worst voluptousness, which is an hydroptic, immoderate desire of human learnings and languages—beautiful ornaments to great fortunes; but mine needed an occupation. . . .[24]

Donne, despite his ability to flatter the great outrageously in an attempt to find a patron, was never "incorporated into the body of the world" as a poet, and was eventually forced to turn to the church and find his occupation as the Dean of St. Paul's.

Edmund Spenser, the most professional of the new poets, remained a poet throughout his life but never quite achieved the status or the ensured social position as a poet that he sought. The story is told of him taking his poetry to Sir Philip Sidney and being kept waiting in the great man's anteroom—because Sidney was engrossed in reading Spenser's poetry. Whatever its truth, the story does dramatize the reality of Spenser's situation, and throughout his life his "deliberately and professionally compounded"[25] poetry was written to win favor of the rich and the powerful in the court and the great houses. His greatest work, *The Faerie*

24. Edmund Gosse, *Life and Letters of John Donne* (New York: Dodd Mead, 1899), 1: 191. Quoted partly in Danby, p. 21.

25. Danby, *Elizabethan and Jacobean Poets*, p. 35.

Queene, was a national epic about England's legendary King Arthur and his knights, and about its reigning Queen Elizabeth, Gloriana, designed to glorify the nation and please its rulers. But despite this great service, Spenser's success in gaining patronage was only partial, and while the support of Sidney, Leicester, and Raleigh did obtain him a secretaryship, land in Ireland, and a pension of fifty pounds a year from the queen, he was eventually burned out of Ireland and died still trying to raise money from his patrons.

Even Ben Jonson, so certain of his importance as a poet in some ways, betrays a lifelong anxiety about the nature of his art and his identity as a poet. After a youth spent as a bricklayer, soldier, and actor, he began to work as a hack writing for the public theater and gradually became a distinguished playwright, the favored poet of a king, and a literary dictator. Despite his lack of a university education and his involvement in the despised theater, his aggressive nature asserted from the beginning his own genius and the crucial importance of poets and poetry to the nation. Though never a great popular success in the theater like Shakespeare or Beaumont and Fletcher, Jonson did succeed in imposing his view of the importance of poetry on a number of rich patrons, and eventually became, as Danby says, the "poet–oligarch" in whom "poet and the patron . . . confront each other as equals."[26] His ultimate patron was King James, whose laureate he became, and who employed him for many years as official writer of elaborate court entertainments, the masques, which manifested the power and magnificence of the absolute monarch. But his success did not save Jonson from an old age of sickness, neglect, and near destitution; and his continuing belligerent efforts in his plays, poems, and criticism to maintain the superiority of his own art, in both public theater and court, against popular tastes make clear the fact that he never succeeded in finding

26. *Ibid.*, p. 43.

a way as a poet of being "incorporated into the body of the world."

When he died in Stratford in 1616, William Shakespeare was a wealthy property owner and a distinguished citizen of the town and the kingdom, and both his financial prosperity and his reputation were the direct results of his success in finding a way in which to incorporate himself as a poet-playwright into the body of the world. He made money in the theater, and he made a name for himself there, by fitting his art to the actual circumstances in which he wrote, working in his theater and with his actors to produce a type of play which satisfied his own high conception of the poet's art, at least to some extent, as well as the varied tastes and interests of the audience in the public theater. His success in the world in adjusting art to the actual conditions of production in the theater reflects an even more profound success in redefining the image of the poet in a way that accorded with the circumstances in which writers like himself actually worked, as the older Petrarchan and Sidnean images did not. It was these circumstances which forced a change in the conception of the poet and his poetry, and before a new image of the poet could appear, these circumstances and their effects upon poetry had to be understood and absorbed into the growing new conception.

Shakespeare was engaged in this examination of the actual conditions in which he wrote throughout his long career in the theater, and by looking at the *Sonnets* and the various plays-within-the-plays in this oeuvre, the points at which he most openly raises and answers questions about the playwright's art, I hope that it may be possible to follow the course of his thinking about his status as a poet in the theater. The obvious place to begin is the *Sonnets* where, whenever they may have been written, he uses a dramatic monologue to present the characteristic situation of the new poets like himself in the 1580s and 1590s, seeking the support of a patron by writing the type of courtly poetry fostered by patronage, but forced eventually to earn a living by "public means." The *Sonnets* depict and justify the transition from courtly poetry to the theater, but the professional theater which came into being in the late Elizabethan period was largely unexplored country for the artist, and a poet in search of an understanding of just who he was and what he could achieve in this new medium had to look carefully at the way in which his plays related to actors, audiences, the public, the state, the older traditions of playing which his theater inherited and, finally, to that strange building, the playhouse in which his plays were performed.

All these matters concerned Shakespeare at all times in his career, but he seems to have been specially concerned with one or the other aspect of theater at particular times. I have tried to follow what appears to have been his own emphasis by concentrating first on what he has to say about actors and audiences, moving on to the question of theater's effect on the commonwealth, and passing last to his reflections on traditional theatrical form and playing style, and the playhouse. In order to make clear the way in which these various realities affected and influenced the playwright's conception of his art, I have provided at the beginning of each chapter a description, as brief as possible, of the theatrical and historical situation in which the artistic questions arose. I hope my more learned readers will bear with me in these summaries of well-known facts, many of which they themselves have made known, and accept their necessity in establishing the relationship of artistic questions to social and theatrical realities.

Seen from the other side, from the artist's point of view, the continuing self-conscious explorations of the nature of theater in Shakespeare's works take shape as a gradual emergence of the dramatic poet out of the play until he at last stands clearly defined, a new dominant image of the poet. This poet does not appear clearly in Shakespeare's early plays, taking only blurred and indirect form as the Prince of Navarre in *Love's Labour's Lost*, the nobleman who arranges the pretense for Christopher Sly in *The Taming of the Shrew*, Petruchio in the same play, or Oberon, the king of the fairies in *A Midsummer Night's Dream*. Hamlet in his play and Edgar in *King Lear* are much clearer images of the dramatic poet, but in the end they too drop back into their plays as characters rather than emerging distinctly as playwrights who control the play and stand outside its action. Only in Shakespeare's last play, *The Tempest*, does a figure emerge, in the magician Prospero, who while still not openly and directly called a playwright is nonetheless unmistakeably an image of the poet in the theater, controlling almost entirely the plot of his play. This solid image apparently could not appear until Shakespeare had confronted and found some way of assimilating to his art all the conditions of playing which so complicated the situation of the poet writing for the theater and made it impossible for him to live out the heroic role of the Petrarchan poet or the courtly role of Castiglione and Sidney. Once the new conditions had been faced and accommodated, then, and apparently only then, could Prospero appear and a new image be created of a poet who uses public means to create theatrical illusions which reveal and change the world.

But the place to begin, as I have said, is with the *Sonnets*, where that mysterious figure of the poet, emotionally attracted to an aristocratic, courtly past represented by the young patron, but fatally drawn to a complex and sensuous Dark Lady, gives us our first shadowed image of what it meant to be an Elizabethan professional poet writing for the public theater.

2

From the Great House to the Public Theater

Shakespeare's *Sonnets* and the Failure of Patronage

The new professional poets of the late sixteenth century found themselves in a sharply contradictory situation. On the one hand, the dominant image of the poet, on which they had to model themselves if they were to be considered, or to consider themselves, true poets was that of the sophisticated amateur like Sidney—easy in manner, polished in style, idealistic, treating poetry as but one part of an active and elevated life. But the reality of their lives made the achievement of this ideal an impossibility, for they lacked the required means and social position to sustain this poetic role, and they were professional writers by necessity, training, and temperament. If they wrote for the printer or for the new public theaters in search of a living, they marked themselves with the stigma of print, pandering to the tastes of a mass audience, the sale of talent for vulgar fame and money, and ceased to be true poets. Patronage was the only social institution available to mediate this contradiction, providing the poets, at least in theory, with the gifts and official appointments needed to enable them to write their poetry and still live out the role of the gifted amateur and man of affairs.

We have as yet no complete study of literary patronage in Shakespeare's England, but all the evidence we do have suggests that the institution did not work very well for poets.[1] In earlier periods when there were far fewer writers, they were largely accommodated as retainers of the court and the aristocratic great families, often living in the household or, more frequently, as priests and officers of the church.[2] Chaucer was a customs official connected with John of Gaunt, Duke of Lancaster, while Petrarch was in lay orders and a dependent of the powerful Colonna family. But with the English Reformation, the church ceased for a time to provide livings for writers, and the Tudor court and a new class of gentry and aristocracy who had been enriched by the dissolution of the monasteries and were dependent for their existence on the favor of the prince became the primary patrons of literature. The Tudor monarchs, with the model of various European courts before them, well understood the use to which artists could be put to glorify their reigns and to support the ideology of the centralized, regulated state; but in a time of considerable change, patronage never seems to have been systematized and woven into the social system

1. The most complete study of literary patronage in Elizabethan England is Eleanor Rosenberg, *Leicester, Patron of Letters* (New York: Columbia University Press, 1955). Rosenberg argues that the patronage system did in fact work and offers strong proof for her position, but it is notable in her argument that it was the historians, theologians, translators, and writers on science and the practical arts who seemed to profit most from the arrangment, while the poets obviously had a much more difficult time of it, as Danby shows. Miller takes up this question in detail in chapter 4, "Patronage," in his *The Professional Writer in Elizabethan England*, and demonstrates conclusively that only a few poets—Spenser, Daniel, Drayton, Jonson—derived substantial amounts from patronage, and even they never found fully satisfactory arrangements.

2. For a discussion of patronage in earlier times, see Karl J. Holzknecht, *Literary Patronage in the Middle Ages* (Philadelphia: University of Pennsylvania Press, 1923).

thoroughly enough to provide poets and those wealthy enough to support them with a clear understanding of the mutual responsibilities of the two parties and the values which could be realized by both through patronage.

Maecenas provided the classical model of the patron, and a few great families, most notably the Sidneys and their kinsmen, the Herberts, the Earls of Pembroke, tried to live up to this noble ideal; but the historical record for the most part bears out Spenser's lament that "*Mecoenas* is yclad in claye, / And great *Augustus* long ygoe is dead."[3] The poets complain regularly that the patrons to whom they address their works, often without being encouraged to do so, fail to understand the value of poetry, are niggardly in their response, do not carry out promises or pay bequests, and in general offer words of praise rather than solid rewards for services rendered. On the other hand, the practices of the poets in seeking patrons are not particularly edifying either. They were regularly capable of a kind of sycophancy difficult to accept in our time, such as is found in Donne's praise of Elizabeth Drury in his "Anniversaries," of which Jonson sourly but aptly remarked to Drummond that "If it had been writ of the Virgin Mary it had been something." Even Shakespeare was capable of the kind of excessive flattery which appears in his dedication of *The Rape of Lucrece* to the earl of Southampton,

The love I dedicate to your lordship is without end; whereof this pamphlet without beginning is but a

3. *The Shepherd's Calendar*, "October," 61–62. For collections and discussions of the evidence of the dissatisfaction with patronage and its generally disordered state, see D. Nichol Smith, "Authors and Patrons," in *Shakespeare's England* (Oxford: Clarendon Press, 1916), 2:182–211; F.P. Wilson, "Some Notes on Authors and Patrons in Tudor and Stuart Times," in *Joseph Quincy Adams Memorial Studies*, ed. James G. McManaway, Giles E. Dawson, and Edwin E. Willoughby (Washington, D.C.: The Folger Shakespeare Library, 1948), pp. 553–61; and Patricia Thomson, "The Literature of Patronage, 1580–1630," *Essays in Criticism* 2 (1952):167–84.

superfluous moiety. The warrant I have of your honorable disposition, not the worth of my untutored lines, makes it assured of acceptance.

But this kind of "princepleasing" is only a modest indication of the scrambling of too many poets for too few patrons which caused Spenser, after dedicating *The Faerie Queene* to Elizabeth, to add seventeen sonnets addressed to various distinguished men of the realm, and which led other writers to print new title pages with dedications to different men for different copies of the same book in the hope of extracting payment from each. The situation at its worst was not much different from that described satirically by Pope in *The Dunciad* over a century later,

> There marched the bard and blockhead, side by side,
> Who rhym'd for him, and patroniz'd for pride.
>
> [IV, 247–48]

The written evidence of the difficulties of patronage corresponds to the facts of the poets' lives, for there is not, I believe it is accurate to say, a single case of a totally satisfactory poet-patron relationship in the time of Elizabeth and James. Even those poets like Spenser, Jonson, Drayton, and Daniel, who enjoyed considerable patronage, were never themselves finally uncritical of the arrangement, and none ever quite found in it the security and the poet's place in the world they needed and desired. Ideally, patronage was what Shakespeare termed it in *Timon of Athens*, "the magic of bounty" (1.1.6), but in actuality it seems to have been about as unsatisfactory and unpleasant as the relationship he dramatizes in that play where the poet is an abject sycophant and self-seeker, a contriver of hypocritical moral allegories, who abandons his patron when his wealth is gone and seeks him out once more when he finds gold again. Timon, the patron, is little more attractive, for he accepts the poetry dedicated to him, and rewards it extravagantly, only because it praises him and contributes to his reputation for magnificence. Of its content or its quality he knows and cares nothing.

In *Timon* the failure of patronage is but one briefly sketched part of a more general social breakdown on all levels, but in his *Sonnets*, Shakespeare explores, as no other writer of his time did, the complex attitudes and social realities which underlie the age's constant complaints about the miserliness and philistinism of the patrons and the lack of merit and unseemly greed of the horde of poets. It is more usual to approach the *Sonnets* as an expression of the deepest feelings about love, friendship, and time, than as an exploration of patronage. But the poet-patron relationship forms the framework or social setting within which the psychological and moral issues are explored.

Modern criticism has chosen to focus on the psychological and moral elements as expressions of universal and timeless human feelings, neglecting the social context in which they appear. This is right in a way, for during the course of the *Sonnets* the interest in human motivation and the strange turns of human nature become the central issues of the sequence; but even as they do so they reflect back upon and explain the failure of the framing patronage relationship. It is the characteristic Shakespearean situation, in which the exploration of the psychology underlying and shaping social institutions becomes more interesting than the institutions themselves. *Lear* begins, for example, as an attempt to explore the failure of kingship and the old order depending on it, but the explanation rapidly becomes more fascinating than the institutions it is designed to explain. Nevertheless, the explorations of the depths of human nature in *Lear* do finally constitute a most profound commentary on the passing of the old order, and similarly the explorations of friendship, love, and lust in the *Sonnets* tell a great deal about why patronage failed and the meaning of that failure.

The dedication of the *Sonnets*, either by Shakespeare or the publisher Thomas Thorpe, ''To the only begetter of / these ensuing sonnets / Mr. W.H.," alerts us to the situation within the poems in which a wise and talented older poet of humble fortune addresses sonnets to a handsome young nobleman which offer him all the rewards a poet could give in exchange for a patron's bounty: praise, fame, the reputation of being a sponsor of learning and the arts, and support for the patron's interests and values. Praise is probably the first and most powerful appeal to a patron, but in order to be truly effective, praise must be offered in such a way as to be fully pleasing without appearing to be exaggerated. The Poet of the *Sonnets* is extraordinarily adroit in phrasing his praises of the young man so that they seem to be not flattery but merely graceful compliment, or even the truthful description of a beauty of such extraordinary quality that it will not be believed by those who have not seen it:

> If I could write the beauty of your eyes,
> And in fresh numbers number all your graces,
> The age to come would say, "This poet lies,
> Such heavenly touches ne'er touched earthly faces."
>
> [17]

The Poet always manages to praise the young man's youth, beauty, and family extravagantly, even fulsomely, while always damping down the suggestion of flattery by the cleverness or gracefulness of the phrasing, mixing the praise with mild reproof, praising while pretending not to, or warning the young man not to be too fond of praise even as the Poet crams him with it. The very form of the address to the patron, the sonnet, is an adroitly indirect compliment which silently associates the young man with the most prestigious of poetic forms and with the ideal beauty which, though in female form, was the traditional subject of the sonnet sequence.

No man has ever been praised more thoroughly or more skillfully than the young man in the *Sonnets*—too much so for most modern tastes—and at the same time aristocratic social concerns and the moral values of his class are presented and their importance insisted upon and demonstrated. Family responsibilities are frequently referred to in rebukes to the young man for letting "so fair a house fall to decay" (13) and lacking the proper sense of family duty in "Seeking that beauteous roof to ruinate, / Which to repair should be thy chief desire" (10).[4] Critics have always been somewhat puzzled by the stress on the young man's marrying and begetting in the *Sonnets*, but one of the major public issues throughout Elizabeth's long reign had, after all, been the question of her marriage and the bearing of a child who would guarantee the continuation of Protestant rule in England. What was of concern to the nation was of vital concern to great families as well, especially during a "crisis of the aristocracy" when,

> exceptionally large numbers of new families were forcing their way to the top, exceptionally large numbers of old families were falling on evil days and sinking into obscurity. There were 641 gentry families in Yorkshire in 1603; by 1642, 180 of these had died out in the male line or left the county, while 218 had first become armigerous, had come into the county, or had set themselves up as cadet branches. This represents a disappearance and replacement of more than one family in four in a space of forty years.[5]

4. "Roof" and "house" are, of course, primarily metaphors for the young man's person, but in the context of the concerns of a noble house they, like many other similar images, inevitably evoke their literal meanings as well.

5. Lawrence Stone, *The Crisis of the Aristocracy 1558–1641*, abridged edition (London: Oxford University Press, 1967), p. 23. "The Crisis of the Aristocracy," both the term and Stone's marshalling of the facts, is the best description we have of that particular aspect of Tudor and Stuart history to which Shakespeare was himself most sensitive. It was, I think it fair to say, his primary subject in many various forms in his plays, which regularly deal with the crisis and passing of an old order, and it is central to the *Sonnets* as well.

In urging the young man to marry and produce children, the Poet is dealing directly with an issue of primary concern to the wealthy families who might patronize a poet, and he pictures directly and powerfully the familiar sight in the English countryside of the ruined castles and obliterated brass funerary monuments which gave realistic urgency to his theme and to the concerns of noble houses for marriage and procreation:

> When I have seen by Time's fell hand defaced
> The rich proud cost of outworn buried age,
> When sometime lofty towers I see down-razed,
> And brass eternal slave to mortal rage;
> . . . .
> When I have seen such interchange of state,
> Or state itself confounded to decay,
> Ruin hath taught me thus to ruminate. . . .
>
> [64]

One of the most important services a writer can render a patron is to provide his immediate social concerns with a metaphysical basis which transforms class values into an ideology. This is what Vergil did for Augustus and Spenser for the Tudor court, and the *Sonnets* achieve the same end by putting aristocratic social responsibilities and modes of life against the background of the titanic and destructive force of "Devouring Time," that "oblivious enmity" which wrinkles all beauty, sluttishly "besmears" the works of men, yellows the pages of the poet, eats away the land, rolls the world around in its seasons and its ages, and rots the body in the grave until it becomes "the prey of worms." Time's desolation is never farther away in the *Sonnets* than the rapidly changing faces and fortunes of men or than the turn of seasons which always brings about

> That time of year. . .
> When yellow leaves, or none, or few, do hang

Upon those boughs which shake against the cold,
Bare ruined choirs where late the sweet birds sang.

[73]

It is against this fear that marrying and begetting children and all the other elements of the aristocratic ethos take on value. Beauty itself, vitality, friendship, faithfulness, generosity, modesty, and above all love—the major moral themes of the *Sonnets* and the principal values of the aristocratic Elizabethan way of life—are virtues because they help "Honey breath hold out / Against the wrackful seige of batt'ring days."

Family and the moral life are the chief defenses against the oblivion of time, but fame can also defeat time, and fame is the gift of the great poet. Eleanor Rosenberg remarks that, "the patron's desire for fame and the writer's unique ability to bestow fame continued to appear in dedications as the primary explanation of patronage and of literary activity,"[6] and at many points in the *Sonnets* the Poet reminds his patron of the extraordinary real value of his services which guarantee, as no other art can, that the individual and the name of the family will "still shine bright" in the "black ink" of his lines.

Not marble, nor the gilded monuments
Of princes, shall outlive this pow'rful rhyme,
But you shall shine more bright in these contents
Than unswept stone, besmeared with sluttish time.

[55]

In order to confer fame on its patron, poetry has to be able to guarantee that it will endure the ravages of time and carry the image of the patron and his values on into the future. The only evidence that a poem can offer of its durability is its own artistic greatness, and a patron is likely

6. Rosenberg, *Leicester, Patron of Letters*, p. 7.

to judge this matter in a relatively conservative way, requiring appropriately conventional subject matter and style. In Shakespeare's case that meant the style recommended by *The Courtier*, the style which enacted the mores of the aristocratic courtly world. Although the Poet in the *Sonnets* speaks of his "tongue-tied Muse," his poems are remarkable for the ease and grace with which they flow—"Honie-tong'd Shakespeare." The music runs smoothly and sweetly, mastering difficult turns and phrasing complex ideas without ever a falter of that "golden quill" which the poet denies that he possesses. This is *sprezzatura* of a kind never seen before or since in English poetry, and it is the perfect verbal enactment of that gracefulness, ease of manner, and regularity which were so highly prized by the courtly world and so central to its art. The same grace carries over into the choice of language—elegant, smooth, slightly elevated without being pedantic, occasionally faintly archaic. A witty playfulness constantly expresses the required intelligence and ingenuity in puns, clever phrasings, variation of meanings on a repeated word, striking metaphors, and the quietly ostentatious use of nearly every known rhetorical figure. This is High Renaissance art of "polished form," which finds its most elaborate expression in what the Poet calls "invention," the application of comparisons of a familiar kind in ingenious extended ways. Courtly poetry was brought in the *Sonnets* to its highest fulfillment, and any perceptive patron should have seen that this was poetry which was indeed capable of conferring fame on its subject. It is one of the ironies of literary history that the poems have lived while the name of the patron has been lost.

Both the patron and the Poet in the *Sonnets* are ideal, and in this fictional situation patronage should work perfectly. But it does not, and the reasons why it fails and the ways it fails offer an understanding of what Shakespeare understood to be the practical and the essential difficulties with the institution. These sonnets differ from the conventional sonnet sequence not only in taking a patron rather

than a "painted beauty" for their subject, but in trans-
forming the usual static repetition of praise and hopeless
love into a developing plot, which brings with it complica-
tions that ultimately destroy the patronage relationship. The
progress of the plot is spotty and difficult to follow, but its
main outlines are clear.

At first the Poet is content to praise the young man's
remarkable beauty and urge him to marry and produce
children, but the sensitive Poet's admiration of his subject
gradually carries him to an intense involvement with the
young man, and he begins to praise him for his own sake,
without further concern for whether he marries or not. The
relationship grows more intense, much too hot even for
Elizabethan ideas of friendship, and though in Sonnet 20 the
poet explicitly denies homsexuality—"since[Nature] pricked
thee out for women's pleasure, / Mine be thy love, and thy
love's use their treasure"—a distinctly erotic quality continues to complicate the relationship. Physical love is never
admitted, but it is always there as a possibility. At first the
young man seems content with the older Poet's admiration,
though separation, some "sensual" straying, and the differences of age and fortune cause difficulties. The first
serious trouble comes when the young man seduces or is
seduced by the Poet's mistress; but though the Poet is
shocked—"yet thou mightst my seat forbear" (41)—he
recognizes that the young man's beauty was an overwhelming temptation and passes the event off with ironic courtly
wit,

> But here's the joy: my friend and I are one;
> Sweet flattery! Then she loves but me alone.
>
> [42]

But the young man becomes increasingly careless of the
Poet's company and feelings—"From me far off, with others
all too near" (61)—and the sensitive and self-doubting Poet
begins to realize his own jealousy and the young man's

indifference. The Poet begins to get a bit shrill at times, doubts the value of his poetry, looks into himself and reflects on his ugliness, his age, and the bitter treatment a rough world accords to men of little fortune. Gradually his suffering forces him to feel the full truth of some of the poetic clichés he had earlier used so easily, and he begins to know that his love, like all other things, is indeed hostage to time and to universal decay, that "nothing stands but for [Time's] scythe to mow" (60).

But the Poet's suffering does not affect the young man, who wades deeper into a life of vice and attracts a rival poet to sing his praises. Gradually the Poet in his growing despair accepts the fact that in the young man, as in so much else in the world, the attractive and the ugly are not separable but fatally intertwined, "How like Eve's apple doth thy beauty grow" (93). But though "Lilies that fester smell far worse than weeds" (94), the Poet is unable to make a clean break on moral grounds, and the relationship limps along, now hot, now cold, always more complicated, until three years have passed and another crisis occurs.

This time the Poet himself is the sinner, and his confession of a "vulgar scandal," sexual in nature, forces him to look deep into the complexities of his own nature and the strange convolutions of love. He realizes that the young man may now feel the same "hell of time" which the Poet earlier felt when he was betrayed, but he now also finds "limbecks foul as hell" in his own mind. Foulness, he comes to understand, makes fairness sweeter, transgression makes return more pleasant, and "better is by evil still made better" (119). Despite his moral shame, the Poet, with a last look over his shoulder at his earlier world—"O thou, my lovely boy" (126)—now turns his attention entirely to a Dark Lady, who immediately proves her fatal power by seducing the young man as well. The Poet's love for the Dark Lady is of an extraordinarily complex nature, unlike the simple admiration and the unqualified love he at first gave the young man. He honestly knows that the lady with her dark complexion and her less than perfect features—"My mistress' eyes are nothing like the sun"—is not beautiful as the world accounts beauty, and he knows that she is, like himself, an artist who paints over ugliness, "Fairing the foul with art's false borrowed face" (127). And yet in his passion he finds her intensely beautiful at times and is willing to "swear beauty herself is black" (132). As he watches her play the "virginal" he is overwhelmed with love, but in a moment more he is plunged into loathing of his own lust, "perjured, murd'rous, bloody, full of blame, / Savage, extreme, rude, cruel, not to trust" (129), and realizes that sexual love is madness which leads only to the most painful disappointment,

> Had, having, and in quest to have, extreme;
> A bliss in proof, and proved a very woe.
>
> [129]

At times she loves him, entices him, and seems to pity him, but then she spits out hate, and he in savage response advises her to at least pretend to love him lest he slander her and destroy her reputation. But worse, the Dark Lady is married—"thy bed-vow broke" (152)—and her affairs with the Poet, described in explicit terms of rising and falling flesh, and with the fair young man are only a few of her conquests. She is, crudely, "the bay where all men ride," and "the wide world's common place" (137). And yet, despite knowing all this and despising his own involvement with her, the Poet cannot break free. He remonstrates, curses himself, forgives, doubts his own senses and his sense, tries to laugh the passion away with grotesque jokes such as celebrating the triangle in terms of conventional love poetry; but he cannot escape. He ends in a condition which a later psychologist has aptly called "knots," where he and the Dark Lady, mutually fascinated and mutually repulsed by themselves and one another, tell each other a complicated set of interlocking lies which each needs to hear from the other in order to support their vanities:

When my love swears that she is made of truth,
I do believe her though I know she lies,
That she might think me some untutored youth,
Unlearnèd in the world's false subtleties.
Thus vainly thinking that she thinks me young,
Although she knows my days are past the best,
Simply I credit her false-speaking tongue;
On both sides thus is simple truth suppressed.
But wherefore says she not she is unjust?
And wherefore say not I that I am old?
O, love's best habit is in seeming trust,
And age in love loves not to have years told.
Therefore I lie with her, and she with me,
And in our faults by lies we flattered be.

[138]

As a love scene this belongs not to the sonnet tradition nor to courtly poetry, but to Cressida's Troy, Hamlet's Elsinore, or Cleopatra's Egypt, and the plot of the *Sonnets* has progressed from an essentially lyric to an essentially dramatic conception of life, which Patrick Crutwell describes in the following way,

As the sequence proceeds, the texture of the poems . . . shows a slow thickening, an increasing complexity. . . . The simple, lyrical, undramatic appealed to, and wrote for, the courtly Renaissance world and the taste which grew from it, whose attraction . . . the young Shakespeare felt strongly; the multiple, critical, dramatic was alien to that world, its true home was the London theater.[7]

7. *The Shakespearean Moment and Its Place in the Poetry of the Seventeenth Century* (New York: Random House, 1960), pp. 8, 26.

It is possible to see in the plot movement of the *Sonnets* from the young man to the Dark Lady a somewhat oblique dramatization of all the major historical difficulties encountered by Elizabethan poets seeking patronage: the untrustworthiness of patrons, the intense competition among rival poets to attract patrons by means of novel styles, the difference between the social status of patron and poet, and the failure of poets and patrons to establish a situation of mutual understanding and support. But the real failure of patronage in the *Sonnets* results from the inability of the institution and the courtly type of poetry it fostered to take into account the realities of human nature and the complexities of human relationships which are discovered as the sequence proceeds, and which are imaged in the Dark Lady.

Throughout the *Sonnets* there is a tension between the style of poetry required by patronage and the real feelings and complexities which the poem discovers. How could a poet praise a patron without reservation, even when he is so atractive as the young man, when in the course of time he turns out to be so vain, changeable, corruptible, and even trivial?[8] How could a poet maintain the proper respectful distance from a patron when he finds himself deeply involved with and emotionally dependent upon him? How could he promise fame to his patron when he begins to realize that poetry, like all other things, is subject to destroying time? How could he teach the proper moral ways of living, when values turn out to be so ambivalent and complex? And how could he be certain of his own authority when he himself turns out to be so uncertain, so various in feelings and attitudes, so unexpectedly full of contradictions? Other poems of patronage simply ignored such questions as these and went on resolutely praising patrons and promising fame, but Shakespeare's *Sonnets* test the poetry of

---

8. On the ambivalence of the Poet toward the patron, see William Empson, "They That Have Power," in *Some Versions of Pastoral* (Norfolk, Conn.: New Directions, 1960), pp. 85–112.

patronage against reality, find it untrue, and abandon the patron to follow the Dark Lady.

But it is not only the appearance of the Dark Lady and all she represents that complicates the situation. The poet's own self-conscious sense of himself and the nature of his art also intrude upon the ideal situation of courtly poetry. We are watching in the *Sonnets* the birth of the professional poet out of the sea of anonymity, and as the sequence proceeds, he gradually emerges as the dominant character. At the beginning of the *Sonnets*, in keeping with the traditions of patronage and courtly poetry, the subject, the young man, is the focal point. The Poet, when he is not merely an impersonal voice, plays out the required courtly role of artistic modesty, deprecating his "slight muse" and "pupil pen," and gives the young man credit for whatever virtue there may be in his poetry. But for all his beauty and attractiveness, we never quite get a full-faced view of the young man. Instead, it is the poet who gradually comes alive, as in Velasquez's painting *Las Meninas*, where the formal subjects of the picture, the king and queen of Spain, appear only dimly in a mirror on the background wall, while the center of the piece is filled by the painter and the observers. In a painting everything we see is, after all, the work of the painter, and Velasquez is simply giving full and open statement to this fact by putting an image of himself near the center of *Las Meninas*. In narrative poetry the only voice we hear is that of the poet, and in the *Sonnets* Shakespeare realizes this implicit condition of his art by accumulating details which gradually create a portrait of the artist, the character I have been calling "the Poet," and positions him at the center of the poem. *Las Meninas* and the *Sonnets* both shift the emphasis from the ostensible subject of art to the making of art, from mimesis to poesis, from the patron whom the artist serves to the professional artist who creates art.

The poet's name is Will (135). He is older than the young man he praises—"forty winters" are mentioned in Sonnet 2—and he feels old enough, "Beated and chopped with tanned antiquity'' (62), to reflect, often in a rather sentimental way, on the inevitable soonness of his death. He is intensely sensitive about his humble origins and his low social position, complaining frequently that Fortune has barred him from "public honor and proud titles" (25) and forced him to live "In disgrace with Fortune and men's eyes" (29). He has known "the lack of many a thing I sought" (30), suffered the loss of love, and seen good friends go to the grave. "Made lame by Fortune's dearest spite" (37), he has been exposed to the harsh realities of the world and, like Hamlet and Lear, learned something of the hypocrisy of the world and the way in which wealth and ruthless power overwhelm simple virtue;

> Tired with all these, for restful death I cry,
> As, to behold desert a beggar born,
> And needy nothing trimmed in jollity,
> And purest faith unhappily forsworn,
> And gilded honor shamefully misplaced,
> And maiden virtue rudely strumpeted,
> And right perfection wrongfully disgraced,
> And strength by limping sway disabled,
> And art made tongue-tied by authority,
> And folly (doctorlike) controlling skill,
> And simple truth miscalled simplicity,
> And captive good attending captain ill. . . .
>
> [66]

His situation and experiences have made him gentle, courteous, careful, and extremely sensitive to his defects of character and his unattractive appearance. But beneath the good manners and modesty, requisite in a poet writing for a patron, pride and powerful ambitions are at work, and he longs to be

> like to one more rich in hope,
> Featured like him, like him with friends possessed,
> Desiring this man's art, and that man's scope. . . .
>
> [29]

But then, in a characteristic turn, he rejects his own envy, "Yet in these thoughts myself almost despising." But "all frailties that besiege all kinds of blood" (109) are at work in his nature, and in spite of his modest condition, "self-love" is so "grounded inward" in his heart that he can think "no face so gracious is as mine, / No shape so true, no truth of such account. . ."(62).

Nowhere does the individuality of the Poet appear more clearly than in his self-consciousness about the nature and value of his own art. Unlike the ideal courtly poet who concealed his personality and art beneath a surface of modesty and effortless ease, this poet constantly betrays his professionalism by his interest in and discussion of poetic matters. He tries to maintain the required courtly stance of a casual amateur, but at times the full pride of a professional in his work breaks through the modest pose and blazes forth in boasts that his own great poetry is immortal and can confer immortality upon its subject: "So long as men can breathe or eyes can see, / So long lives this, and this gives life to thee"(18). In his pride, he can also be bitter that circumstances force him to sell "cheap what is most dear" (110).

The professionalism appears also as a persistent curiosity and desire to talk about various philosophic and technical issues important to a practising poet: the value of tropes, the relation of idea and image in poetry, the interaction of art and nature, the right use of poetry, comparisons of various poetic styles and the difficulty of changing a personal style once it has been set and perfected. He spends an entire sonnet, 59, on the ancients and the moderns, wondering if the old writers—"Since mind at first in character was done"—wrote equally well as or better than those of the present day, and if they did, why then should the moderns labor so "for invention" only to repeat what has been already done? He spends another sonnet, 76, discussing the sameness and conventionality of his poetry, which only dresses "old words new" and produces poems which sound so much alike "That every word doth almost tell my name." He is concerned and troubled by the appearance of a popular new style—probably of the type we now call "metaphysical"—and analyzes its "new-found methods," "compounds strange," "variation or quick change," and "new pride." Nor is this the only new style on which he ponders, for his patron attracts another poet, and the "proud full sail of his great verse" (86) is divinely inspired by nightly visitations from an "affable familiar ghost" and spirits who teach the rival poet "to write / Above a mortal pitch." This high heroic verse—it sounds like Marlowe or Chapman—intensifies the Poet's sensitivity about his own admitted lack of divine inspiration and the sameness of his subject matter and his style—"I must each day say o'er the very same" (108).

The Poet suffers many of the defects which must have complicated patronage in Shakespeare's time: the poverty and powerlessness of the poet in dealing with a wealthy patron, his low social status, the consequent uncertainty about the value of his art, the tension of being a professional trying to maintain the role of an amateur, and the simultaneous humility and fierce pride in his own abilities. But the nub of the matter is finally the professional's sense that poets and poetry are more interesting than patrons and the values of their class. This is what the *Sonnets*, by their concentration on the Poet and his interests and thoughts, finally say, and this shift in focus makes the poetry of patronage finally impossible.

The Poet's shift in interest from the patron to poetry parallels the shift already discussed from the conventional situation of courtly poetry to the complex realities of the world, and these changes of interest inevitably force a shift in poetic style as well. The tradition of courtly poetry is brought to its highest fulfillment in the *Sonnets*, its old ideas dressed in the brightest clothes they would ever wear; but ironically, even as the heights are achieved, the Poet begins to weary of and doubt the style he uses so perfectly. At first the doubts are expressed only briefly and in passing, but by Sonnet 76, uneasiness finds almost unqualified expression in a poem that states both the nature of the conventional type of poetry and the source of its problem:

> Why is my verse so barren of new pride,
> So far from variation or quick change?
> Why with the time do I not glance aside
> To new-found methods and to compounds strange?
> Why write I still all one, ever the same,
> And keep invention in a noted weed,
> That every word doth almost tell my name,
> Showing their birth, and where they did proceed?
> O, know, sweet love, I always write of you,
> And you and love are still my argument.
> So all my best is dressing old words new,
> Spending again what is already spent. . . .

Although the Poet is not yet willing to abandon his old subject and the style in which he praises it, there is here a tiredness with the sameness of the themes and style of his poetry, and by Sonnet 108 he can be quite explicit about the tedium of telling over the glories of beauty, love, and friendship in the same terms,

> What's in the brain that ink may character
> Which hath not figured to thee my true spirit?

His invention is exhausted, however, because the subject on which it must express itself is exhausted as well, and a little later he explicitly renounces and mocks the style he has worked in so successfully because he now recognizes that it is not adequate to the reality of the Dark Lady, who has become the true poetic subject.

> My mistress' eyes are nothing like the sun;
> Coral is far more red than her lips' red;

If snow be white, why then her breasts are dun;
If hairs be wires, black wires grow on her head.
I have seen roses damasked, red and white,
But no such roses see I in her cheeks,
And in some perfumes is there more delight
Than in the breath that from my mistress reeks.
I love to hear her speak, yet well I know
That music hath a far more pleasing sound.
I grant I never saw a goddess go;
My mistress when she walks treads on the ground.

[130]

The plot of the *Sonnets* in its movement from the young man to the Dark Lady leads, as we have seen, from a lyric to a dramatic conception of life, from simplicity and certainty to complexity and ambiguity, and the Poet moves in the same direction from the great house to the public theater. In the earlier portions of the sequence there are hints that the Poet works in the theater. He uses particularly precise theatrical metaphors—"As an unperfect actor on the stage, / Who with his fear is put besides his part" (23)—he refers to wearisome traveling in the country in a way that suggests actors on tour, and he has known the weight of "art made tongue-tied by authority," which may refer either to the censorship imposed on the theater or to the authority of correct neoclassical critics like Sidney. But it is not until Sonnet 110 that it becomes fairly certain that the Poet is one of those "learned Lawreat masters of England" who "for lacke of Patrones (0 ingratefull and damned age) . . . are soly or chiefly maintained, countenawnced, and patronized" by the "witty Comedians and stately Tragedians (the glorious and goodlie representers of all fine witte, glorified phrase, and queint action)."[9]

9. Francis Meres, *Palladis Tamia* (1598), in *Elizabethan Critical Essays*, 2:313.

Alas, 'tis true I have gone here and there
And made myself a motley to the view,
Gored mine own thoughts, sold cheap what is most dear,
Made old offenses of affections new.
Most true it is that I have looked on truth
Askance and strangely; . . .

These lines may be and have been read as a denunciation of patronage itself which forced he Poet to sell "cheap
what is most dear,"[10] but the details of this and the following
sonnet suggest the public art of the theater more strongly
than the more private art of writing poetry for a patron. The
reference to the "motley" costume of the clown who was so
prominent a figure on the English stage forces the interpretation in the direction of the theater and strengthens the
association of "gone here and there" with the provincial
tours of the Elizabethan professional companies in times of
plague and during the summer season when their London
theaters were closed. "Goring"—which carries its original
sense of "dirtying," as well as "wounding"—of the Poet's
thoughts and selling "cheap what is most dear" combine to
suggest a type of writing like working for the public theater,
which was generally thought of, though not by Meres, as a
degrading form of business and popular entertainment, an
unfit activity for idealistic, high-minded poets.

10. See James Winny, *The Master-Mistress, A Study of Shakespeare's
Sonnets* (New York: Barnes and Noble, 1968), pp. 80–85. Winny, like so
many other commentators on the *Sonnets*, absolutely rejects any connection of Sonnets 110 and 111 to the theater. I can only record my own view,
shared with many other readers, that the theatrical interpretation fits in
perfectly with the development from the lyric to the dramatic conception
of life in the *Sonnets* as a whole, and that, while recognizing that the Poet
does not represent Shakespeare in all respects, it is impossible and wrongheaded to deny altogether the knowledge that he was the ultimate author
of the poems and that his experience as a playwright and actor therefore
provide us to some degree with the necessary context in which to
understand the *Sonnets*. This is one of those instances where it seems to
me entirely proper to interpret somewhat ambiguous details in terms of
what we know about the author.

In the next sonnet, 111, the Poet goes on to explain that while his name and nature may have been stained by writing for the public, probably in the theater, that it was—as indeed it was in Shakespeare's case—his poverty and his lack of high birth, the deficiencies he has earlier complained of, that have forced him into his corrupting trade:

> O, for my sake do you with Fortune chide,
> The guilty goddess of my harmful deeds,
> That did not better for my life provide
> Than public means which public manners breeds.
> Thence comes it that my name receives a brand,
> And almost thence my nature is subdued
> To what it works in, like the dyer's hand.
>
> [111]

Although the official death of patronage is not usually said to have come until a century and a half later with Samuel Johnson's letter to Lord Chesterfield, Sonnet 111, with its apparently unanswered plea for the necessary support from a patron—"Pity me then, and wish I were renewed"—is one of the crucial documents in the long history of the artist's turn away from patronage to the public marketplace as a source of support. It announces that, however much they may dislike it, poor but talented writers can earn their livings writing for the public, in this case for the theater, selling "cheap what is most dear." It also makes clear that a different audience and different financial support will produce a new kind of art which will look "on truth / Askance and strangely," for "public means" do "public manners breed." But the *Sonnets* do not merely show the change from patronage to the marketplace as a sad necessity of life, they justify it as well by demonstrating that only a realistic dramatic style can truthfully present the complexities and ironies of actual existence. The movement of poetry from the great house to the theater was, in the mind of the greatest dramatist of the age, necessitated not only by certain social changes but by the professional artist's pursuit of truth. Near the end of the *Sonnets*, the Poet exclaims,

> Love is too young to know what conscience is,
> Yet who knows not conscience is born of love?
>
> [151]

Conscience—in the sense of "knowing" as well as in the moral sense—grows out of experience of the intense relationships of love and leads to the discovery of the contrast between physical beauty and the moral weakness of the young man, the Poet's own personal and moral imperfections, the awareness that everything, even love, does change in time, and the baffling feelings for the Dark Lady. All these create a growing sense of complexity, relativity, the intermixture of good and evil, the simultaneous existence of logical opposites, which are central to the dramatic conception of life. The young man and the Dark Lady are not only characters but symbols as well of two views of life, and two kinds of art:

> Two loves I have, of comfort and despair,
> Which like two spirits do suggest me still;
> The better angel is a man right fair,
> The worser spirit a woman colored ill.
>
> [144]

The fair young man as he first appears is the Muse of courtly lyric poetry fostered by patronage: open, clear, idealized, beautiful, changeable rather than complex in nature, polished in manners, the inheritor of a great tradition, aristocratic and male. The Dark Lady is the Muse of theater: illicit, darkly mysterious, sensual, infinitely complex, beautiful and ugly, common and public, the source of pleasure and of pain. As Crutwell says,

> Shakespeare's complaint that his nature had been "stained" by his bread-winning at the playhouse was

true in a way which perhaps he did not know: in his raid
[in the *Sonnets*] on the world of politeness and "gentility" and essential simplicity, he took over with
him—he could not help it—the complex ironies of the
professional dramatist.[11]

It is impossible not to see close correspondences between the life of William Shakespeare and the portrait of the
Poet in the *Sonnets*. Shakespeare, too, was a poor young man
who came to London, probably in the late 1580s, to make a
living for himself as an actor and playwright in the public
theaters. And he too tried, at least for a time, to cultivate the
role of the courtly poet, writing fashionable erotic poetry like
Venus and Adonis and the *Rape of Lucrece*, dedicated to and
designed to please a noble patron, the earl of Southampton.
By applying for a coat of arms which permitted him to style
himself "William Shakespeare, Gent." he, too, tried to avoid
being "mistaken for a writer of broadside ballads . . . the
risk the middle-class poet ran who ventured into print" by
fortifying "every possible claim . . . to gentility."[12] He
circulated his "sugred *Sonnets* among his private friends,"[13]
in manuscript and perhaps did not involve himself in their
eventual publication in 1609,[14] thus showing the required
indifference toward print of the courtly poet. But while it
seems inescapable that Shakespeare was, in the *Sonnets*,

11. *The Shakespearean Moment*, p. 27.
12. Saunders, "The Stigma of Print," p. 155.
13. Meres, *Palladis Tamia*, p. 317.
14. The decision by many scholars that Shakespeare was not involved
in the publication of the *Sonnets* has led in turn to an assumption that he
did not revise the poems or arrange them in a completely consistent order.
The only evidence given, however, for questioning the order of the poems
is always a critical decision that they do not make sense, i.e., tell a
coherent story, in the order in which they were originally printed. Since
my own argument in this chapter depends on accepting, at least roughly,
the order of the 1609 edition, I would like to record here my view that
there are really no solid bibliographical grounds for questioning that
order, nor any critical need to do so since the poems do form, in my
opinion, a loose but perfectly coherent plot.

reflecting his own actual circumstances as a writer and expressing the problems he had with patronage and the role of the courtly poet, it seems equally clear that, in a characteristic way, he was not so much writing a chapter of his own autobiography as depicting in a much more general way the experience of a transitional generation of poets from an amateur to a professional status, and from patronage to the marketplace as a source of support. Whatever longings Shakespeare may have had to be a fashionable and courtly amateur, he was and remained primarily a professional actor and playwright, and the *Sonnets* are finally, whatever their nostalgia for old courtly ways, an apology for the necessity of working in the public theater. A necessity not only because patronage failed to work socially and economically, but because a new class of self-conscious professional poets had appeared for whom the importance of art lay not in its ability to serve an established aristocratic social system so much as in its power to capture in a dramatic, not a courtly style, the complex reality of human actions and motivations.

The *Sonnets* justify the theater and the participation in it of professional writers with a high view of the importance of their art like Shakespeare, and they are the necessary first step toward the construction of a new image of the poet in accordance with the facts of the changed conditions of writing. But the step from the great house to the theater is taken, it should be noted, with great reluctance at leaving a golden past, and with grave doubts about the nature and value of the new medium in which the poet must now realize his art. As the Muse of the theater, the Dark Lady promises as much pain as pleasure, at least as many lies as truth, and perpetual ambiguity and uncertainty. It was exactly in this problematic way that Shakespeare seems to have understood his dramatic art, and his plays contain a long record of a continuing effort to deal with and explain a medium which remained always something less than fully satisfactory.

3

"A Little O'erparted"

Actors and Audiences in
The Taming of the Shrew, Love's Labour's Lost,
A Midsummer Night's Dream, 1 Henry IV

The theater is a public art and the playwright therefore works under vastly different conditions than the poet. What the playwright has to say must be said through the voices and styles of the actors, and it must be played on a particular stage in a particular theatrical building, all of which affects the playwright's original intentions. The play's ultimate statement will in large part be what those who produce it make of it, and its meaning will finally be determined by the response of an audience made up of many different people of widely varying interests and capabilities. When the performance ends the play disappears as if it had never been, and if it is played again it will take a new form from adjustments made in the playhouse, from the presence of new actors, and from the inevitable changes in the tone and style of performance from day to day. No play is ever the same play twice running. Even if the play is eventually fixed in print it is always, even under the best of circumstances, difficult to establish the text which represents the "true" play, and any printed text will always be only the bare bones of something that was designed for the stage and can achieve its full reality only in the transitory color, light, voices, and movements of the theater. Furthermore, because the production of a play involves large numbers of people and the use of expensive materials and property, the theater inevitably becomes entangled in complex economic issues. Being a public affair, openly staged out in the world before the eyes of large numbers of its citizens, a play also affects society and must face the question of its relationship to the state and its governors, who inevitably try to use and control such a powerful means of propaganda.

All these conditions of theater work together to diminish the importance of the playwright's role in the creation of art and to place into question the existence of the work of art in any absolute, ideal sense. It is difficult for a playwright to conceive of himself as a heroic poet like Petrarch or a courtly poet like Sidney, and equally difficult for him to think of his play as a perfect artifact, wrought from his own vision and standing forever as an unchanging image of truth and beauty. A courtly sonneteer like Shakespeare's Poet might boast that "Not marble, nor the gilded monuments / Of princes, shall outlive this powr'ful rhyme," (55) but a writer for the theater knows that no man and no playwright

> is the lord of anything—
> Though in and of him there be much consisting—
> Till he communicate his parts to others.
> Nor doth he of himself know them for aught
> Till he behold them formèd in th' applause
> Where they're extended. . . .
> [*Troilus*, 3.3. 115–20]

The very nature of theater as a public art forces these realizations on any playwright at any time, but the actual conditions in which Elizabethan plays were written and produced intensified the playwrights' awareness that a poet and his plays were only a part of a much larger grouping of people, traditions, and social forces interacting in complex ways to produce theater. A poet like Petrarch or Sidney could, because of his favored social position and freedom from economic pressures, see poetry as high art, ideal truth, and the expression of personal genius. An Elizabethan playwright working for money in the public theater, having to consider the interests of his audience and the nature of his playing company and physical theater, could be far less certain that his work was art, that it expressed his own genius, or that its value extended beyond today's performance.

The sons for the most part of lower-class artisans and middle-class tradesmen—scriveners, bricklayers, cobblers, glovemakers—in many cases the first in their families to have received even a grammar school education, the Elizabethan playwrights were the first of that long line of poor but gifted writers—Johnson and Garrick, Gogol, Balzac—who made the mythic journey from the country to the capital city to earn fame and fortune by their art. Patronage did not really function for them, the book trade could not yet adequately support them, and so the surplus of talented young men whose humanist literary educations made the profession of writing seem both important and feasible found employment in the only place they could, the new theatrical repertory companies with their need for hundreds of plays a year.

Robert Greene's *Groatsworth of Wit Bought With a Million of Repentance,* in which he attacks Shakespeare as a mere actor who has begun to "bombast out a blank verse" in competition with his betters, and the academic *Parnassus Plays* written at Cambridge, tell of the indignation that educated authors felt at their treatment in the theater, where most either sank without a trace or became hacks turning out plays as commodities. Only a few really became successful playwrights. We know the titles of over a thousand plays written by identifiable authors between 1590 and 1642, and of these nearly half were written by a group of only twenty-two men who became the real professionals of the theater.[1] Thomas Heywood, the most prolific of this group, wrote or had a hand in two hundred and twenty, but Shakespeare, who wrote thirty-eight, or a little less than two a year during his working life, is more characteristic of the hard-working professional.

The playwrights, at least the better ones, never surrendered their status as poets nor conceded that their plays were less than art,[2] but their plays reveal not certainty but a deep unresolved tension between conceptions of the theater as an unlimited artistic power and as mere clownish spectacle. The magic which Marlowe's great philosopher Doctor Faustus commands is an idealized form of the playwright's ability to transform the world on his stage into the images of desire, producing grapes in winter or bringing Helen of Troy to life. But Faustus sells his soul for this absolute theatrical power, and even he finds in the end that he can create only transitory and unsatisfactory images. The clock strikes twelve as he disappears into Hell to pay with his soul for what have come to seem to him trivial powers, and the epigraph "Terminat hora diem, Terminat author opus" drives home the identification of damned magician with disenchanted playwright. Artistic anxiety is even more openly expressed in Jonson's *Volpone*, where the enormous energy and power of playing appear in perverse form as the rich merchant Volpone, the "great impostor," who acts out a

1. G.E. Bentley, *The Profession of Dramatist in Shakespeare's Time* (Princeton, N.J.: Princeton University Press, 1971). This authoritative book on the conditions in which the playwrights worked is the source of these and many of the facts about the playwrights in the following discussion.

2. David Klein, *The Elizabethan Dramatists as Critics* (New York: Philosophical Library, 1963) culls from the plays of the period a number of the many direct statements about art, which suggest the constant concern of the playwrights with artistic questions and their self-conscious desire to remind the public that the plays were serious works of art. Madeline Doran, *Endeavors of Art* (Madison: University of Wisconsin Press, 1953), provides a good summary of the kinds of major questions about the nature of dramatic art which engaged the playwrights.

pretense of sickness on the curtained stage of his great bed in order to satisfy his lust, his greed, and his desire for power.[3] The Protean ability of Shakespeare's Richard III to change shapes at will, like the actor to whom he is frequently compared, frees him from limits imposed by his twisted body and a desperate time, but he uses his theatrical powers to deceive, to kill, and to attack society.

The theatrical self-consciousness of the Elizabethan and Jacobean dramatists has been much commented upon,[4] and there has recently been a growing reaction against the view that the dramatists, particularly Shakespeare, were so obsessed with critical questions and aesthetics that, whatever the ostensible subject of their plays, all are ultimately "metadrama"—all plays, that is, about the nature of playing. I would agree that the artist's preoccupation with theory and his own role as a poet is predominantly a romantic and postromantic development resulting from the increasingly problematic nature of art in a scientific, utilitarian world. But the evidence is undeniable that the English Renaissance dramatists did concern themselves in their plays in obvious ways with the function of art and the proper nature of playing. They did so, however, at least in the first instance, not because of some deep philosophical commitment to theoretical issues, but out of a need to resolve the very real tensions created by a situation in which the writers' conception of the nature and value of their art did not square with the actual circumstances in which their plays were

3. Jonson's basic "Anti-theatricalism" is fully treated in Jonas A. Barish, "Jonson and the Loathèd Stage," in *A Celebration of Ben Jonson*, ed. William Blissett, Julian Patrick, and R.W. Van Fossen (Toronto: University of Toronto Press, 1973), pp. 27–53.
4. Two recent books which show very clearly the trend to argue that poetic and aesthetic questions are at the center of all Shakespearean drama, even when theatrical matters are not explicitly treated, are: James L. Calderwood, *Shakespearean Metadrama* (Minneapolis: University of Minnesota Press, 1971), and Lawrence Danson, *Tragic Alphabet* (New Haven: Yale University Press, 1974).

written and produced, or with the popular valuation of their work.

The English drama of the Renaissance has for so long been thought of in Romantic terms as the highest of the high arts, the glory of Literature, that it is now difficult to understand in what low esteem plays and stage were held during the great dramatic period in England from the building of the first professional playhouse in London in 1576 to the closing of the theaters by the Puritans in 1642. It was not that drama itself was despised, for the Roman dramatists, and to a lesser degree the Greeks, were studied, admired, translated, imitated, and performed in aristocratic and academic settings. Drama was widely understood, except by the more radical Puritans, who abominated all playing as pagan pretense and idleness, to be a high art with a long tradition of greatness in presenting moral truths and advising princes in memorable and powerful ways.

The theater that was despised, feared, and mocked was a professional theater which evolved during the sixteenth century from mummings and agricultural festivals, the old biblical cycles and public pageants, juggling acts and morality plays, morris dances and courtly entertainments. Professional acting companies formed during the fifteenth century and toured the country, playing on trestle stages in inn yards and public squares, before the screen in great halls of noble houses and guildhalls, in churches and in chapter houses. We have a vivid portrait of such a company in John Marston's play, *Histriomastix*, written about 1599, satirical in intent but furnishing some idea of what touring companies in earlier and later times probably were like. Several idle artisans, Gulch, Clout, Belch, Gut, and Incle, combine to form a playing company. They hire as their playwright the hack poet, Master Posthaste, call in a scrivener to draw up articles, choose the name of "Sir Oliver Owlet's Men" and the badge of "an owl in an ivy bush" for their company. They assemble a repertory of plays to fit every type of audience and set off with a wardrobe of new costumes,

obtained on credit, to tour the countryside, singing their song:

> Some up and some downe, ther's Players in the towne,
>> You wot well who they bee:
> The summe doth arise, to three companies,
>> One, two, three, foure, make wee.
> Besides we that travell, with pumps full of gravell,
>> Made all of such running leather:
> That once in a weeke, new maisters wee seeke,
>> And never can hold together.[5]

When Sir Oliver's Men reach a town they send out one of their players to the square, where he mounts the steps of the market-cross and cries out a play to be given in the town hall at three o'clock in the afternoon. Soon afterwards they are invited to play in the hall of a local noble where, after putting on a grotesque morality play, *The Prodigall Child*, they are paid three shillings and four pence. Inept as they are, they prosper and become proud, until they fall athwart the law and all of them are pressed into service and shipped overseas to fight in foreign wars.

With the construction in 1576, just to the north of the London wall, of the first of many permanent playhouses, the public theater began to stabilize in London—though the companies were still forced frequently to tour—with daily performances, distinguished star actors, professional playwrights, and a more solid financial base. As Christopher Hill makes clear, this new professional theater, however closely it may have been related to older theatrical traditions, constituted a revolutionary change in the conditions in which art was produced:

> The way in which capitalist relations came to pervade all sectors of society can be illustrated from an industry

---

5. *The Plays of John Marston*, ed. H. Harvey Wood (Edinburgh: Oliver and Boyd, 1939), 3:264. No line numbers are supplied in this text.

not often considered by economic historians—the entertainments industry. Before 1577 theatrical productions had been small-scale, once a week at most, either private performances by the dependants of a great lord or the amateur productions of a community, whether guild, Oxford or Cambridge college, or one of the Inns of Court. The financial genius of James Burbage brought playing from a small-scale private enterprise to a big business. The Theatre and the Curtain were both opened during 1577 [*sic*] with the object of producing plays to which the general public would be admitted on payment. The capital for the Globe was provided in part by the actors themselves, on a joint-stock basis. For prudential reasons the patronage of the royal family or of leading aristocrats was retained (under an Act of 1572 actors not so protected could be treated as vagabonds), but henceforth the profit motive prevailed. The drama was the first of the arts to be put on sale to the general public. Larger theatres brought bigger profits if the dramatist could draw his public. This created exciting new possibilities for writers, though capitalism had its drawbacks too. 'Should these fellows come out of my debt,' said the biggest theatre-financier of all, Philip Henslowe, under James I, 'I should have no rule with them.' It was this quite new commercialism in the theatre, plus the fact that the new theatrical buildings were outside the City and so immune from control by the City authorities, that led to the so-called 'Puritan' attack on the stage—which in origin was not Puritan at all and was restricted to an attack on the commercial stage.[6]

Like all popular theater, this was primarily an actor's theater, and the actors organized themselves in the manner

6. *Reformation to Industrial Revolution*, vol. 2, 1530–1780, of The Pelican Economic History of Britain (Harmondsworth: Penguin Books, 1969), p. 89.

common in other business enterprises of the day, as a guild or company of master craftsmen, setting standards of workmanship, limiting membership, and training their successors. But as Hill reminds us, "We should certainly not be sentimental about guilds in our period, whatever they may or may not have been earlier. They were usually controlled by oligarchies, and were often employers' rings."[7] In the tradition of the craft guild system, each of the principal actors had his apprentice, bound to him for the usual period of seven years, during which time he was provided for by the master craftsman and taught his trade. These apprentices supplied the company with the necessary extra actors, and also, with their high voices and beardless faces, played the female roles. If times were prosperous, the numbers of the company would be swelled by hired actors who worked for a straight wage, and by the necessary technicians: bookkeepers, musicians, gatekeepers, sound-effect men and the like. A well-to-do company installed in a London theater might employ as many as between sixty and eighty men, where the earlier traveling groups consisted of only four to six players.

The presence in an acting company of eight or ten permanent players, who as "sharers" had controlling financial interest in the company, tended to set the acting techniques and styles of the company. These were repertory companies in the true sense, and each of the players had a standard type part and a personal acting style. In the Lord Chamberlain's Men, after 1603 the King's Men, William Shakespeare's company, the major actor was Richard Burbage who played the leading parts—Hamlet, Lear, Antony, Othello—from his first known appearance in the theater around 1590 to his death in 1619. The clown of the company was originally Will Kemp, the most famous comedian of his day. Jigs and other dances were his trademark, and at one time he jigged all the way from London to

7. *Ibid.*, p. 91.

Norwich. Encouraged by this success, he set out to dance his way over the Alps to Italy, but gave up the attempt, though he did go on to Italy and played for a time in the *Commedia dell' Arte* there, and his easy transition to this extemporary theater suggests that there must have been a good deal of stock farce and improvisation in the English public theater. Shakespeare was himself an actor in his company, as well as resident playwright, but of his acting line we know little, though tradition has it that he played older parts such as the Ghost in *Hamlet*.

When an Elizabethan dramatist wrote a play he had to keep in mind the abilities and preferences of such actors and the acting capabilities of the particular company. If the company did not have a boy capable of playing female parts really well, then it would be folly to write plays such as *Romeo and Juliet*, *Antony and Cleopatra*, or *The Winter's Tale*, all plays in which there are leading female roles. As long as Kemp was the company clown, the fools in the plays performed by his company were of the buffoonish, slapstick type—Gobbo or Dogberry. After Kemp left the company and Robert Armin began playing the clown's part, the fools became more subtle, ironic and melancholy—the Fool in *Lear*, and Feste in *Twelfth Night*.[8]

But the actors controlled the plays they played in in even more direct ways. Shakespeare enjoyed a favored relationship with the King's Men as an actor, a sharer, resident playwright, and part owner of the Globe and Blackfriars theaters in which his company played. But something like the more usual way in which plays were written is suggested by the manner in which Philip Henslowe, a builder of theaters and an early entertainment entrepreneur, and his son-in-law, Edward Alleyn, the leading tragedian of the Admiral's Men, contracted for their plays

---

8. The argument for the tailoring of the plays to the actors' styles is worked out in detail by T.W. Baldwin, *The Organization and Personnel of the Shakespearean Company* (Princeton, N.J.: Princeton University Press, 1927).

from such freelance writers as Henry Chettle, Thomas Heywood, Anthony Munday, and Thomas Dekker. Henslowe, whose income depended partly on the gate at his theater, would pay a playwright a fee ranging from a few shillings to two pounds for a rough outline of a plot which had theatrical possibilities. The actors would then look at the outline and suggest changes. Then Henslowe would hire from one to as many as five playwrights to go to work on the play, presumably assigning each to work on his specialty, though he at times seems to have simply given each an act to write.

At this stage in the proceedings, Henslowe would advance to his author or authors a certain amount of money, perhaps as much as a pound, and when the play was completed and accepted, he would pay the rest of the money due, if the needy playwrights had not, as was often the case, obtained advances to live on in the meantime. With the finished play in hand, the actors would again go over it, and if there were parts they did not like, or which they thought could be bettered, Henslowe might pay perhaps ten shillings to one of the original authors for additions and changes, or he might call in a new specialist to write some more dialogue or add a spectacular scene. Not only were new plays constructed in this manner, but old favorites owned by the company were frequently refurbished in similar ways to bring them up to date.

The control of the actors over their plays was ultimately almost absolute. The acting company commissioned the plays, paying on the average about six pounds in the 1590s, which, as Gerald Bentley points out, was a fairly good wage when ten pounds was a schoolmaster's annual wage and forty shillings the usual payment by a printer for a book. Later the rate rose to as high as twenty pounds, but even in the 1590s a busy playwright could make twenty to thirty pounds a year. In return for these payments, however, the delivered play became the absolute property of the players, and they could and did change the play in any way they wished. Radical changes were likely in a popular play which remained in repertory for several years, and these changes often were made by a resident play-fixer, an actor beefing up a part, or by some outside writer, not necessarily the original author. As a result of all this changing in the theater, the text of a play was never really fixed, and many plays have consequently come down to us in such radically different versions that it becomes genuinely questionable whether we can say that a play ever had an absolute form or we can establish a "true text." Furthermore, it seems not to have been in the interest of the players to print the successful plays in their repertory lest their availability for reading reduce attendance at the theater; and so the plays were guarded rather carefully and often found their way to the printer only when the texts were pirated, usually in a corrupted form, or when some disaster such as the breakup of a company or the prohibition of playing because of plague forced a company to sell off its assets.

Dramatists thus found themselves in a new economic and artistic status as writers for wages, or as entrepreneurs who produced goods for the entertainment marketplace and depended for a living on the saleability of their commodity. It was difficult to think of what they produced under these circumstances as art expressing a poet's genius and winning him eternal fame by its perfect and permanent form. Instead, the actual facts of production defined plays as an amusement product, written on commission, often put together in collaboration, shaped to the styles and interests of particular actors, constantly changing form in the theater, used up in production, and dependent on pleasing for a moment the tastes of "Dukes and ambassadors, gentlemen and captains, citizens and apprentices, ruffians and harlots, 'Tailers, Tinkers, Cordwayners, Saylers, olde Men, yong Men, Women, Boyes, Girles, and such like.' "[9]

9. Stephen Gosson, *Playes Confuted in Five Actions*, quoted in R.A. Foakes, "The Profession of Playwright," in *Early Shakespeare*, Stratford-Upon-Avon Studies 3 (New York: St. Martins Press, 1961), p. 11.

It was this audience on which the income of the theaters and of the playwrights depended, and no poets had previously faced and had to please a large public of this particular kind and with this degree of power over art. The courtly poet had purposely limited his audience to a small, select group, and the new professional poets of the latter sixteenth century, like Spenser or Donne, had also addressed only a patron and a small circle of men with similar aristocratic tastes. But the English playwrights now found themselves paid and judged by a group very different from the small intellectual and social world which had previously been the audience for art.

The Elizabethan theater audience was a large one. Alfred Harbage in his authoritative study, *Shakespeare's Audience*, concludes that the capacity of the Elizabethan public theaters was between 2,500 and 3,000, and that the average daily attendance in 1595 at one London theater, the Rose, was slightly over 1,000. Greater London then had a population of about 160,000, and Harbage estimates that 21,000, or about 13 percent, went to the theater in any given performance week in 1605.[10] The audience seems to have been as various as it was large, but on the exact nature of that variety the evidence and the conclusions which scholars have drawn from it are contradictory. Most of the contemporary descriptions of the audience are written from a hostile, often a Puritan, point of view and portray the "common haunters" of the theater as

> the leaudest persons in the land, apt for pilferie, periurie, forgerie, or any rogories, the very scum, rascallitie, and baggage of the people, thieues, cut-purses, shifters, cousoners; briefly an vncleane gener-ation, and spaune of vipers: must not here be good rule, where is such a broode of Hell-bred creatures? for a

10. *Shakespeare's Audience* (New York: Columbia University Press, 1941), chap. 2, "How Many People."

Play is like a sincke in a Towne, wherevnto all the filth doth runne: or the byle in the body, that draweth all the ill humours vnto it.[11]

Attacks such as this provided the basis for the long-accepted view of Shakespeare's audience as idle apprentices, thieves, whores, young gallants, and a group of people who in general would presumably not have been much interested in art. But in his thorough and convincing survey of the evidence, Alfred Harbage rejects this older view and finds instead "a large and receptive assemblage of men and women of all ages and all classes,"[12] predominantly working class,[13] decent, cheerful, quiet, and capable of understanding in large measure the plays they saw.

> I should guess that the audience as a whole understood and appreciated what it bought and approved. Its approval could not have been easy to win. . . . Shakespeare's audience was literally popular, ascending through each gradation from potboy to prince. It was the one to which he had been conditioned early and for which he had never ceased to write. It thrived for a time, it passed quickly, and its like has never existed since. It must be given much of the credit for the greatness of Shakespeare's plays.[14]

Whatever the exact nature of the audience may have been—and the evidence suggests that it was far more likely

11. Henry Crosse, *Vertues Commonwealth* (1603), quoted in *Ibid.*, p. 4.
12. *Shakespeare's Audience*, p. 158.
13. Ann Jennalie Cook, "The Audience of Shakespeare's Plays: A Reconsideration," *Shakespeare Studies VII*, ed. J. Leeds Barroll (Columbia: University of South Carolina Press, 1974), pp. 283–306, looks at the evidence again and concludes that what Harbage called the "working class" did not in fact make up such a large proportion of the theater audience as he thought. In her view, the audience seems to have been more middle and upper-middle class, therefore presumably less democratic and popular in its education and tastes.
14. *Shakespeare's Audience*, p. 159.

to have been a cross-section of London, with a predominance of educated and intelligent people than "a broode of Hellbred creatures"—there is no question that Shakespeare pleased it with plays that only rarely pandered to low or debased tastes. We know this not only from the fact that he prospered and became a rich man from his involvement with the theater, but also from the contemporary tributes paid him as the greatest and most popular of the English playwrights. A real sense of his popularity and the excitement that the plays created in the theater can be felt in the lines Leonard Digges wrote for inclusion in the 1640 edition of Shakespeare's poems:

> So have I seene, when Cesar would appeare,
> And on the Stage at half-sword parley were,
> *Brutus* and *Cassius:* oh how the Audience
> Were ravish'd, with what wonder they went thence, . . .
>   let but *Falstaffe* come,
> *Hall, Poines*, the rest you scarce shall have a roome
> All is so pester'd: let but *Beatrice*
> And *Benedicke* be seene, loe in a trice
> The Cockpit Galleries, Boxes, all are full
> To heare *Maluoglio* that crosse garter'd Gull.

Shakespeare was remarkable among the playwrights of the time for the close relationship he maintained with his fellow actors in the company which produced his plays, and for the popularity he enjoyed with his large audience from early on in his career. But his success in dealing with these two new and crucial factors in the creation of art did not apparently make him any the less wary of them or the less concerned about the part they had to play in the theater if his plays were to achieve the effects he conceived as being within the possibility of great dramatic art. References in his plays to actors and to acting are on balance negative, and the audiences he portrays on stage are never ideal but always something less than satisfactory in their behavior and their comprehension. Of all the English dramatists, Shakespeare seems to have been torn most severely between the conception of his plays as high art and as mere entertainment, and Philip Edwards rightly calls him "the experimenter, engaged in a continuous battle, a quarter of a century long, against his own skepticism about the value of his art as a model of human experience."[15] He left us no direct critical statements about the issue, of course, but instead explored the question in his plays by allowing his characters and his scenes to state and to pose again and again the fundamental theatrical problems. His concerns and his developing understanding of the theater are imaged most sharply and summarily in the little internal plays, the plays-within-the-play, which, as Leslie Fiedler puts it, allow a play to provide "a history of itself, a record of the scruples and the hesitations of its maker in the course of its making, sometimes even a defense or definition of the kind to which it belongs or the conventions which it respects."[16] Shakespeare's scruples and hesitations about the effect of actors and audiences on his plays are focused in three of his early plays, *The Taming of the Shrew*, *Love's Labour's Lost*, and *A Midsummer Night's Dream*, where internal plays are staged in such a way as to reveal the nature of the doubts a practicing playwright had about the ability of actors to present, and audiences to understand and be properly moved by, the poet's "most rare vision."

But it is always well to remember that Shakespeare is the most elusive of writers, the most difficult to find in his

15. *Shakespeare and the Confines of Art* (London: Methuen, 1968), p. 10.

16. "The Defense of the Illusion and the Creation of Myth, Device and Symbol in the Plays of Shakespeare," in *English Institute Essays, 1948*, ed. D.A. Robertson, Jr. (New York: Columbia University Press, 1949), p. 74. The history of this theatrical device is given in F.S. Boas, "The Play Within the Play," in *A Series of Papers on Shakespeare and the Theatre by Members of the Shakespeare Association* (London: Oxford University Press, 1927), pp. 134–56; Arthur Brown, "The Play Within a Play, An Elizabethan Dramatic Device," *Essays and Studies*, n.s. 13 (1960): 36–48; and in Robert J. Nelson, *Play Within a Play, The Dramatist's Conception of His Art: Shakespeare to Anouilh* (New Haven: Yale University Press, 1958).

plays. The nature of the theatrical medium and his own ways of thinking and working combined to create plays which do not show us clear, direct statements of set moral or intellectual attitudes,, but rather offer us the mystery of human motivation concealed behind words and actions, and a multiplicity of points of view and ambiguous events which encourages a variety of interpretations and meanings. If we are to find in his plays what Shakespeare himself thought about the theater, it must be by an elaborate process of triangulation, or by trying to catch a fleeting reflection in an extended series of mirrors. By isolating the various plays-within-the-play it is my hope to set up such a series of mirrors that will show us something of what Shakespeare thought of his own art in relation to the conditions of theatrical production. The mirrors agree in reflecting continuing concern about the effectiveness of actual theater in achieving the results of which it is ideally capable, and they thus suggest that Shakespeare was always troubled by the problems of theatrical production. But the images in the mirrors are complex, and rather than showing a romantic artist's complete despair with his medium, they reflect both a wary concern for the dangers of production and a continuing positive belief in the enormous power of theater in general, and of his own plays in particular.

The Taming of the Shrew is a theatrical tour de force in the use of the play-within-the-play, consisting of plays set within plays and actors watching other actors acting, seemingly extending into infinity.[17] All the world *is* a stage in Padua, where the theater is the only true image of life. In the outermost frame-play a drunken tinker, Christopher Sly, is picked out of the mud by a rich lord and transported to his house. A little pretense is arranged, purely for amusement, and when Sly awakes he finds himself in rich surroundings,

17. Richard Henze, "Role Playing in *The Taming of the Shrew*," *Southern Humanities Review* 4 (1970): 231–40, describes in detail the extent of playing in *Shrew* and its ability to transform some of the characters, but not Sly, who in his opinion remains the irredeemable old Adam.

addressed as a nobleman, obeyed in every wish, and waited on by a beautiful wife.

At this point a group of professional traveling players appears to the sound of trumpets to provide entertainment in the great house. They are warmly welcomed and fed, and are asked to put on a play for the tinker, who is represented as a noble and eccentric lord. The inner play about the taming of the shrew, which the players then perform, is in turn filled with many other instances of playing. Young men disguise themselves in order to marry beautiful young girls and get their fathers' money, while servants play masters and masters play servants, all for pleasure and profit, in the most literal sense of those famous Horatian terms. Petruchio arrives "to wive it wealthily in Padua" and finds that theatrical methods alone will enable him to transform the beautiful and wealthy Kate from a cursed shrew, useless to herself and anyone else, into a loving and happy wife. Wooing as playing begins at once as Petruchio pretends that Kate is in all ways the very opposite of what in fact she is:

> Say that she rail, why then I'll tell her plain
> She sings as sweetly as a nightingale.
> Say that she frown, I'll say she looks as clear
> As morning roses newly washed with dew.
>
> [2.1.170–73]

His acting intrigues Kate, at least to the extent that she agrees to marry him.

Petruchio's greatest play is staged on his wedding day when he appears in a fantastic, ragged costume and takes Kate on a wild ride through the rain and cold to an isolated country house where he forces her to fast, to remain awake, and to endure a number of frustrations to her will, all the time pretending that he is concerned only for her well being. Playing is here an instrument of power which enables Petruchio to dominate Kate, force her to play in his play, but it also shows Kate "feelingly" the misery of a household and human relationships in which one selfish will is set absolutely against all others. She gives no indication of having consciously learned the moral lesson that the play's mirror holds up to her, but in order to protect herself and procure the necessary food, clothing, rest, and return to life within the social community, represented by the return from the isolated country house to Padua and her father's home, she herself learns to become a player.

However, the playing has had its effect, even though, as is so often the case in Shakespeare, the "audience" responds with only rudimentary surface understanding of what they have seen and been moved by. Kate has been changed by Petruchio's pretense, even if she does not understand, or at least does not speak of, its full meaning and power, and at the end of the play we see a Kate who can cheerfully say that the sun is the moon or can pretend to be absolutely subservient to a husband's will if domestic tranquility so requires. She has perhaps not been broken to her husband's will, nor even, perhaps, become more sweet-tempered, if generations of actors have interpreted the play properly, but she has at least learned that living and loving both require considerable pretense.

Like opposed mirrors, the inner play of the Shrew and the outer play of Christopher Sly reveal the same truth by reverse means. In both cases some disordered and wasted portion of humanity has been transformed and redeemed by means of a play and acting, but Sly is shown what he might find in a positive sense—a noble life—Kate in a negative—a life of misery and deprivation. In both cases the desired end can be achieved only by play-acting. Kate acts out her understanding dramatically by pretending to obey absolutely and to believe everything Petruchio says, while Sly acknowledges the wonderful powers of art by proclaiming that he is no longer one of those ancient Slys who "came in with Richard Conqueror," but has become something new and wonderful:

Am I a lord, and have I such a lady?
Or do I dream? Or have I dreamed till now?
I do not sleep: I see, I hear, I speak,
I smell sweet savors and I feel soft things.
Upon my life, I am a lord indeed
And not a tinker nor Christopher Sly.

[*Ind.*2. 68–73]

The Shrew dramatizes the traditional Horatian view that the function of comedy is both to please and to instruct, achieving these ends not by directly imitating reality, but by creating exaggerated and distorted images of life which show Sly how wonderful the world could be and show Kate how terrible it could become. The play, however, expands the modest claim of pleasure and profit to suggest that the histrionic art not only instructs in a right and pleasurable way of life but is also itself literally the means of reaching happiness and pleasure, in the theater and in life. Restage the world and the life within it can be utterly changed! Art can make drunken tinkers and savage shrews into noble lords and loving spouses.

The claims for the power of the theater are large and confident in *The Shrew*, but at the same time the play glances uneasily at the real circumstances of the Elizabethan theatrical world in which plays had to try to realize their near-magical powers of transformation. The motives for theatrical performance are no higher than a simple desire for amusement by the nobleman who picks Sly out of the gutter, and the crudest kind of desire for economic profit in the case of Petruchio and the other internal actors. And despite the miraculous transformations achieved by playing, art works its magic without either the actors or the stage audiences fully understanding what happens to them. The chief actor, Petruchio, exults crudely and openly in the wealth he has won and his absolute power over his "audience" wife, while Kate, Sly, and others, the first of Shakespeare's many uncomprehending audiences, are changed radically by their encounter with theater, but without quite knowing what has taken place.

And, of course, there is the possibility that neither Sly nor Kate has really been changed. The play's ironic doubts about the value of theater are considerably extended if we accept the view of many critics[18] that the old play *The Taming of A Shrew* represents not Shakespeare's source but his original play in a corrupt, pirated form, and that the text of *The Shrew* which appears in the First Folio is a later redaction of the older play. In *A Shrew*, the Sly frame-play has a final scene in which Sly is transported back to the mud from which he came and awakes in the morning to worry about how he will explain his night's absence to his wife. But then he remembers the way in which Petruchio had handled Kate and sets off confidently for his home to tame another shrew. The small likelihood of his success points up the gap between art and life and drives home what *The Shrew* only suggests, that plays don't really change life very much.

The Shrew reveals Shakespeare's characteristic stance throughout his career as a playwright in the theater. Theater is an art form, not mere entertainment, and a play proves its right to the status of art by its ability to show men, even if for only an instant, what they and their world might ideally become, and even provides them with a model of how the transformation might actually be wrought. But at the same time, the actual conditions of theatrical production are not as ideal as might be desired, and the doubtful motives and limited comprehension of actors and audiences represent not

---

18. The case for *A Shrew* representing Shakespeare's original play is ably argued by Peter Alexander, "The Original Ending of *The Taming of the Shrew*," *SQ* 20 (1969): 111–16. An important counterargument is made, however, by Thelma N. Greenfield, "The Transformation of Christopher Sly," *PQ* 33 (1954): 34–42, who sees the dropping of the last scene, whoever may have written the original, as an important part of Shakespeare's dramatic strategy of juxtaposing two contrasting worlds—Sly and Art, reality and the play—in such a way as to demonstrate the ultimate power of the imagination.

only the situation the playwright had to deal with in presenting his play in the theater, but the stubborn, intractable nature of reality itself which his illusion had to try to overcome.

The Shrew is, however, on the whole optimistic about the powers of theatrical art; but in another play, written about the same time as *The Shrew*, Shakespeare presents an open image of theatrical failure, showing in some detail the ways in which the wrong kind of acting and audience response can prevent theater from achieving the effects of which it is ideally capable. The action of *Love's Labour's Lost* consists of an almost endless series of artful games and play through which

> Shakespeare explores the dimensions of the play faculty, from charming fripperies to serious products of the imagination: dressing up, disguising, dance, and song in the Masque and Pageant; flirtation and erotic play; the play of language and minds in puns, alliteration, euphuistic rhetoric, and verbal wit, as well as in the manipulated conceits of the love poetry and the tortuous logic of the set speeches; allusions to specific children's games and toys; and the game of the chase, the hunt for "game."[19]

The exploration of the "play faculty" is concentrated in two internal plays, an aristocratic "Masque of the Muscovites" danced by the Prince of Navarre and his companions to woo the Princess of France and her attendants, and a disastrous, bumbling lower-class attempt by several pedants and local clowns to stage a "Pageant of the Nine Worthies" to please and edify the nobility.

Both masque and pageant fail to achieve their desired effects because the actors lack the necessary skills and the

---

19. Louis A. Montrose, "Sport By Sport O'erthrown: *Love's Labour's Lost* and the Politics of Play," *Texas Studies in Literature and Language* 18 (1977): 529.

audiences lack the willingness to suspend disbelief needed to banish reality for a moment and create theatrical illusion. The young nobles who dance in the masque are clumsily disguised and inept, while the young ladies know who the dancers really are all the time and use their knowledge "To dash it like a Christmas comedy," mocking the men out of their pretensions of being Muscovites and true lovers. Reality is even crueler to the actors in the "Pageant," who forget their lines, mispronounce words, misplace accents in their doggerel verse, stumble awkwardly about the stage, and in general demonstrate how hilariously unsuited they are for such heroic roles as those of Alexander and Pompey. The Prince and his companions jeer cruelly at the actors from the audience, and at the most desperate moment of the play an unwelcome outside voice announces that the actor who is struggling to deliver himself of the role of Hector has gotten one of the local wenches with child.

But even as the theater is laughed at for the gap between its high pretensions and its moldy actualities, for the inability of its art to repel a stubborn reality, audience and actors are reminded that plays might succeed if only they would play their parts properly. The young nobles, who hoot and jeer at the bumbling actors in the pageant in a most cruel way, are rebuked directly by one of the actors for their lack of manners—"This is not generous, not gentle, not humble"—and are instructed in a number of subtle and indirect ways that tolerance and understanding of even bad actors is a necessary virtue in an audience. The same warning applies to the young ladies who constitute the audience of the Masque of the Muscovites; for their unwillingness to forget that the masquers are really a group of awkward young men, and to forgive the clumsiness with which they act out their parts, prevents the masque from achieving its aim, a happy ending of resolved sexual conflicts.

But if the audience must cooperate for plays to succeed, so must actors play their roles in a way that encourages

suspension of disbelief and creates the illusion which allows
art to function. Costard, the "rational hind," speaking of one
of his fellow players pretending to be Alexander the Great,
makes clear how crucial it is that actors should play
reasonable subjects in a style in which they are competent,
avoiding the dangers of pride and overwhelming ambition:

> There, an't shall please you, a foolish mild man; an
> honest man, look you, and soon dashed. He is a
> marvelous good neighbor, faith, and a very good
> bowler; but for Alisander—alas! you see how 'tis—a
> little o'erparted.   [5.2.576–80]

The lines remind us that the Prince of Navarre and his
companions have also been "a little o'erparted" throughout
the play. Earlier they had set up an academy in which they
planned to explore the deep truths of philosophy and win
undying fame by perpetual study and abstention from food,
sleep, and the company of women. When the beautiful
Princess of France and her ladies arrrive, the young men at
once begin to play the parts of lovers and poets, with about
as much success as their earlier attempts to play
philosophers and later ones to play Muscovites. The ironic
parallels between this kind of being "o'erparted" in the main
play and that of the actors in the pageant become obvious
when a messenger enters to announce the death of the king
of France, thus bringing *Love's Labour's Lost* to an end by an
intrusion of reality of the same kind that earlier interrupted
the "Pageant of the Nine Worthies" by the announcement of
Jaquenetta's pregnancy.

Since all of life is play-acting, the play seems to be
saying, and since all men are such awkward and o'erparted
players, it behooves members of an audience to treat even
inept actors and foolish plays with the good manners and
sympathy which should be born out of an awareness of their
own deficiencies as fellow players. Such tolerance will help
a play create the illusion needed to bring about the ends

toward which the internal plays in *Love's Labour's Lost* aim: the triumph of love, the reconciliation of opposites, and the expression of good will and the desire to please.

All this is done very lightly. Shakespeare the professional dramatist in a London theater seems merely to be laughing at the performances of amateur players and at the same time indirectly instructing his own players and audience in their proper duties. But despite the easy manner of the playwright, *Love's Labour's Lost* still reveals a deep concern about the uncertain dependence of plays on actors and audiences to create the illusion needed to allow art to deal successfully with that troublesome reality which always impinged so directly and powerfully on the imaginative constructions of a playwright in the public theater. Actors and audiences who refuse to relinquish their own selfish sense of themselves in order to give themselves to the play defeat all the attempts in *Love's Labour's Lost* to shape and direct life to a satisfactory conclusion by means of art of various kinds, including plays. Shakespeare drives home the point, implicating the outer audience at the same time, by allowing his own play to fail in ways that suggest just how difficult it is for art to contain and shape reality.

Love's Labour's Lost is in some ways the most self-consciously "poetic" of Shakespeare's plays, but its extraordinarily rich and playful language is in the end overwhelmed by a reality which its verbal art cannot repulse. Just as the interior plays are invaded and broken off by too strong a sense of reality in the audiences, and by such real facts as Jaquenetta's pregnancy, so is Shakespeare's play invaded by the news of the death of the king of France, which brings the wooing to an end, prevents the usual marriages of comedy, and forces the young men out into the world for a time to learn such hard realities as loneliness, mourning, time's effect on love, and the meaninglessness of witty words in the face of pain and death. The play acknowledges its own chosen failure to bring the plot to the usual happy conclusion of romantic comedy—"Our wooing doth not end like an old play; Jack hath not Jill"—and in doing so expresses its concerns about the ability of the words and forms of art to control reality. As this "great feast of languages" ends, all its wonderful words, which are one of the high points of the courtly poetry of the Renaissance, give way to the simple, repetitive sounds of nature, the cuckoo's monotonous song of spring, sex, and fertility, and the lonely "Tu-whit, Tu-who" of the owl telling of cold, sickness, and death. If art is to impose its bright words and happy ending on this reality, then Shakespeare's actors and audiences will have to play their parts with more understanding and ability than the characters in the play.

In his first decade as a dramatist, Shakespeare seems to have been on the whole optimistic about the power of playing to affect, even in less than ideal circumstances, the real world. He laughs at actors for their clumsiness and audiences for their literal-mindedness, chiding both for their inability to forget themselves and enter fully into the play; but the laughter, while it bears witness to some uneasiness on the part of the dramatist about his theater, seems in many ways merely the graceful modesty of an accomplished and self-assured professional dramatic poet continuing the proud humanistic tradition of claiming high value for his theatrical art. Nowhere is the modesty so complete, and at the same time the claim for the potential value of playing so extensive, as in *A Midsummer Night's Dream*, where Shakespeare dramatizes Sidney's boast that in place of nature's brazen world the poet creates a golden one, that imagination can perceive and art reveal an unseen reality just beyond the range of the senses and of the rational mind. In the *Dream*, art is no longer defined only by its ability to shape and transform an obstinate reality, as in *Shrew* and *Love's Labour's Lost*, but is shown to have an ability to penetrate the screen of the immediate world and reveal an imaginative truth that lies behind it.[20]

20. Richard Henze, "*A Midsummer Night's Dream*: Analogous Image," *Shakespeare Studies VII*, pp. 115–23, discusses the relation of

Again Shakespeare glances, with an amusement that still betrays uneasiness, at the crudities of actors and stage and at the limitations of audiences. No players could be more hopeless than Nick Bottom the weaver and his mechanical friends who, in the hope of winning a small pension, perform the internal play, "Pyramus and Thisbe," to celebrate the marriage of Duke Theseus of Athens to the Amazon queen, Hippolyta. Bottom's company, a parady of the amateur players and provincial touring companies who performed in aristocratic houses on special occasions⟨is so literal-minded as to require that the moon actually shine on the stage, that the wall through which Pyramus and Thisbe speak be solidly there, and that the actor who plays the lion assure the ladies in the audience, lest they be afraid, that he is only a make-believe lion. The deficiency of imagination which lies behind such a laughable conception of theater, carries over into the playing style of the actors as well.⟩Their stumbling rant, missed cues, mispronounced words and lines, willingness to converse directly with the audience, doggerel verse, and general ineptitude, constitute a playwright's nightmare and completely destroy any possibility of creating the necessary illusion. As one critic describes it:

> actors do intervene between audience and playwright. The play clearly indicates that intervention, and, as Bottom demonstrates in his failure as an actor, the actor, like the playwright, must be able both to perceive and to express the imaginative idea if the play is to be successful. For Bottom's audience to imagine a credible

---

Shakespeare's concept of the imagination in *Dream* to older theories, such as Sidney's, and concludes that "Shakespeare's poet is less a divine creator than Sidney's" (p. 123), and that his "artist is distinct from other men not in his ability to give form to airy nothing, nor in his ability to ideally imitate, but in his ability to express imaginative forms that all men see" (p. 118). Henze argues his position effectively, but while Sidney may be making more absolute claims for poetic imagination than Shakespeare, both poets are still, in varying degrees, locating the power of the poet in the ability to present a reality beyond the range of normal vision.

Pyramus, Bottom the actor's Pyramus, as well as Bottom the playwright's Pyramus, must be credible. If the playlet is to succeed, both the playwright's and actor's Pyramuses must be believably dead. Long before Bottom rises with his assurances that he is alive, the imaginative expression has been so disrupted that the audience's imaginative perception is prevented. Imagination cannot amend the matter; judgment takes over, and judgment tells us that this is the silliest matter that we have ever heard.[21]

The audience at "Pyramus and Thisbe," Duke Theseus, his queen Hippolyta, and the young lovers who attend them, are socially superior to the actors but little more sophisticated about their proper roles in making a play work. Theseus does understand that, though this may be "the silliest stuff" ever heard, it lies within the power of a gracious audience to improve it, for "The best in this kind are but shadows; and the worst are no worse, if imagination amend them" (5.1.211–12). But the noble audience seems to have little of the necessary imagination, for they violate the imaginative space of the play, which the players have first breached, by mocking the actors, laughing at their tragic efforts, and talking loudly among themselves during the performance. For them a play is only the means to while away a dull wait on their wedding night and, secure in an untroubled sense of their own substantial reality, they can laugh at what unrealistic and trivial things all plays and players are. Theseus, that champion of Athenian rationalism, has already publicly declared that the poet's imagination is no more truthful than the lunatic's delusions or the lover's belief in the perfect beauty of his beloved:

The poet's eye, in a fine frenzy rolling,
Doth glance from heaven to earth, from earth to heaven;

21. *Ibid.*, p. 121.

And as imagination bodies forth
The forms of things unknown, the poet's pen
Turns them to shapes, and gives to airy nothing
A local habitation and a name

[5.1.12–17]

Shakespeare seems to have constructed in *Dream* the "worst case" for theater, voicing all the attacks on drama being made in his time and deliberately showing plays, actors, and audiences at their worst. And since "the best in this kind are but shadows," "Pyramus and Thisbe" seems to indict all plays, including *A Midsummer Night's Dream*, as mere rant of awkward actors and unrealistic dreaming of frenzied poets. But, while admitting the worst, Shakespeare has contrived at the same time to defend plays in a most subtle fashion. Even as Theseus and his friends sit watching "Pyramus and Thisbe," laughing at poetry and plays and actors, they are themselves, seen from our vantage point in the outer audience, only the "forms of things unknown" which the imagination of William Shakespeare bodied forth and gave the habitation of Athens and such odd names as Helena and Hermia, Demetrius and Lysander. The situation is the same as that in *Love's Labour's Lost*, where the scorn for plays is also discredited by showing the audience to be themselves only players, and not such very good ones at that, in a larger play of which they are totally unaware.

This is true in *Dream* in the literal sense that the stage audience is made up of actors in Shakespeare's play, and also in the sense that they have already been unwitting players in another internal play written and produced by that master of illusion, Oberon, king of the fairies. He and Titania between them have earlier managed the lives of Theseus and Hippolyta as if they were unconscious actors in a play, and during the course of *Dream*, Oberon contrives on the stage of his magical forest a little illusion which instructs the young lovers, feelingly not consciously, in the dangers of unleashed passion and brings them at last to a happy conclusion in which every Jack has his Jill. Oberon's magical forest is a

77

perfect image of what a theater might ideally be and do, but even here the most all-powerful of playwrights is subject to the ability of the imperfect instruments through whom he must implement his art, and Puck nearly ruins the play by putting "idleness" in the wrong eyes.

As we in the audience watch Theseus watching Bottom pretend to be Pyramus, the extended dramatic perspective forces us to consider the possibility that we too may be only another player audience on another larger stage. And if this is the case, then the audience is not only once again reminded by the bad manners of the stage audience of the positive part it must play in making theater work, but it is also being told that its own sense of the real may be no more valid than Theseus's. If his rationalistic scorn of plays and players is called into question by his status as only another player, then perhaps our skepticism about Shakespeare's play is equally compromised, for we stand in the same relationship to the things unknown that the imagination of William Shakespeare has bodied forth as *A Midsummer Night's Dream* as Theseus does to "Pyramus and Thisbe." A forest ruled over by a contentious fairy king and queen, a magical love potion which causes love at first sight, a comic trickster like Puck, all are at least as real as a player duke who marries a queen of Amazons, rules over a city named Athens, and believes that a way of thinking called reason shows the truth of things. And they may finally be as real as that "sure and firm-set earth" we take to be our own reality. If *all* the world is a play, then one play may be as true as another; and if the conditions are right, as in Oberon's play but not in Bottom's, then the theater may reveal the true nature of the world and effect its transformation.

The playwright drives home his point in the final scene. After Theseus and Hippolyta and the other couples, Bottom's play finished, make their way to bed thinking that reality reigns again, the stage fills with all those fairies which Shakespeare's imagination created to embody his vision of the beneficent but tricky forces at work in nature, just beyond the range of the daylight eye. Again it is done lightly, the claim half concealed and discounted even as it is so charmingly made, but immediate reality is being heavily discounted and a visionary power is being claimed for the dramatic poet by leaving his fairies in possession of a stage which now extends outward to claim the entire theater and the world beyond as a part of its imaginative realm.

In *Dream* Shakespeare claims for the dramatic poet all the powers which the Renaissance conferred on art, but his image of the theater still acknowledges the crudity and accidents of stage presentation, the clumsiness of actors, the incomprehension of audiences, and the danger that plays may be mere fantasy without much relation to reality. If the play is to work, as he tries to make *Dream* work, and its full powers are to be realized, then actors and audience must accept that they and their "real" world are finally as illusory as a play, are simply another play called reality, and enter with their imaginations into the full spirit of creating between them on the stage an alternate fictional world of faires and lovers which can reveal another aspect of truth.

In Shakespeare's exploration of theater in his plays of the 1590s, the poet-playwright does not himself appear openly but only in some surrogate form of creator such as the Prince of Navarre and his companions, who construct an academy and a masque; or Petruchio, who writes his shrew play as he goes along; or Oberon, who commands the illusory power of the fairy world; or perhaps even the enthusiastic actor Bottom, who is always willing to stretch a part or add a piece of business to the script of the mercifully anonymous "Pyramus." The absence of any direct image of the playwright accords with the actual situation in the public theater, where the playwright and his text remained invisible behind the production of the play. It was the play in performance in the theater before an audience that was the artistic reality, and it is on production that Shakespeare focused his attention in his internal plays, showing always in these early plays a less than ideal situation.

It may be, of course, that in treating the theater in its negative aspects, concentrating on its problems while only implying its successes, Shakespeare was calling attention by contrast to the effectiveness of his own plays and their productions, in which he participated as an actor. He was, after all, a professional writer for what was by all accounts a skillful professional company playing in an excellent London theater, while the players he portrays in his plays are either members of a touring road company or amateurs performing old-fashioned entertainments and dramatizations of "moldy tales" in a pavilion in an open park, the dining hall of a great house, and the presence chamber of a court. No doubt there was some of a professional's feeling of superiority to the amateur in all of this, but these theatrical situations also image, in however indirect or exaggerated a way, the public theater for which Shakespeare wrote. And they make it clear that Shakespeare was profoundly sensitive to the fact that the wrong kind of actors, productions, and audiences could destroy a play, no matter how good the text itself might be.

About the power of plays themselves and their potentially beneficial effects on life, he seems to have been at this time highly optimistic and to have felt that the playwright was not a mere entertainer but a dramatic poet. Playing of the right kind could transform Sly from a tinker to a lord and Kate from a shrew into a loving wife, and at the same time be not merely the image of such transformations but the means by which they might be achieved. In *Love's Labour's Lost*, though frustrated in actual performance, art in all forms including the play has the potential for uniting a variety of people, men and women, nobles and commoners, and adjusting their natural conflicts in such a way as to bring them to a happy ending and provide them with the fame or love they seek. In *Dream* we see the success of art in the world of the fairies where Oberon creates illusions and directs a plot which undoes the tangles and dissolves the hatred and frustration of the young lovers. It is important to note that in these plays art is never seen as some abstract thing far removed from life but always as a force working directly and immediately upon life, changing the world by reconciling opposites and transmuting a difficult reality into the forms that man desires.

But despite the high potentials of playing, it either never quite works in these plays, or it works against odds. The actors are often "o'erparted," like the Prince of Navarre and his companions, or the "Nine Worthies," or Bottom's company, taking on high heroic roles which strain nature and for which their talents are inadequate. Or they are motivated in wrong ways which eventually lead to a bad performance, as Petruchio's greed leads him to overplaying his swaggering style and finally being outplayed by Kate, or as Bottom's bumptious and ill-placed confidence in his histrionic powers makes him want to absorb *all* the parts in the play—"Let me play the lion too"—and leads to him overreaching himself in "a part to tear a cat in." Performances can also be spoiled by actors like Kate as she first appears, or the prince and his companions, or the young lovers, all of whom have too little sense of themselves as actors and play out their parts without any understanding of their status as players. The danger is always a performance like "Pyramus and Thisbe," in which imagination and reality are not sufficiently balanced to create the illusion a successful play requires to work its magic. The ideal seems to be a performance in which reality is neither so openly flouted as to make the play unbelievable, nor rendered so literally as to make it ridiculous, but is balanced with imaginative pretense in such a way as to manifest the purpose of playing itself, the channeling of nature by art into harmonious and satisfactory patterns.

The audiences bear as much responsibility as the players for creating this ideal, and they fail to play their parts as regularly as do the actors. Occasionally they may be taken in and believe in the illusion too completely, as Sly does in believing that he *is* a lord, or Bottom in believing that he is an ass beloved by the queen of fairies. But most often it is an imaginatively deficient audience in these early plays which contributes to the failure of performances by refusing to enter into the necessary pretense. Reality is too real for them, and so the young ladies in *Love's Labour's Lost* will not forget for the moment that the young men in the masque are really only clumsy lovers who a moment ago were pretending to be philosophers. So, too, the audiences at the "Pageant of the Nine Worthies" and "Pyramus and Thisbe" lack the imagaination to understand that they too are actors, and not such good ones, and they therefore do not show the necessary good manners and courtesy which would help to overcome the ineptitude of the actors and make the play a success. Their jeers and mockery not only fluster and discourage the actors but invade and destroy the magical space of the stage where the fragile but powerful illusion of art must work.

All Shakespeare's doubts about the competency of actors and audiences, which continue to appear in his plays to the end of his career, are summarized toward the end of the 1590s in *1 Henry IV* in the little play-within-the-play in the Boarshead Tavern, where Falstaff and Hal perform a brief scene modeled on an old "Prodigal Son" type of morality play. Playing in an old-fashioned style—"in King Cambyses' vein"—Falstaff, "as like one of those harlotry players" as ever Mistress Quickly saw, takes the part of King Henry admonishing his wastrel son Hal. With only a few props—a cushion for a crown, a lead dagger for a scepter, and a jointstool for a throne—he improvises a sonorous speech which reveals the king as a pompous, long-winded, self-righteous figure of fun. Falstaff hams the part up for all it is worth, delighting Mistress Quickly and the rest of the audience in a tavern where plays were often performed in actuality, but his performance does not amuse Hal, who plays for bigger stakes than Falstaff, and he takes over the role of king, delivering a performance which manifests, still with some touches of humor, the awesome sternness and power of a great king. His concluding revelation of the ultimate banishment of Falstaff—"I do, I will"—suggests both the power of playing to reveal the truth and the way in which acting can be used, and will be used, in the coronation scene where Falstaff is actually banished, to instrument that truth.

Falstaff is a fine actor, capable on one occasion of saving his life by pretending to be dead, and life seems to be for him a series of parts played for profit and pleasure: the brave captain, the misled virtuous youth, the wise old councilor, the innocent victim of worldly guile. But he always has something of Bottom in him, playing his roles too broadly and always ignoring, eventually fatally, the full dimensions of the reality he imitates and seeks to control by his acting. His pretenses are always parodies and always delightful, but they never quite tell the total truth, and they usually fail to persuade their audiences entirely.

Hal is ultimately a better actor, whose performances capture more of reality, and are more convincing, not only in the Boarshead scene or his imitation of Hotspur, but in the various political scenes he plays throughout his life: pretending to be a wastrel in order to appear more attractive when he becomes king, or pretending to be the victim of France's plot to deny him his rightful heritage as king. His strength as an actor seems to originate in his full acceptance of the fact that he is an actor, manifested in the beginning in his soliloquy in the Boarshead—"herein will I imitate the sun"—and fully acknowledged on the night before Agincourt when he accepts kingship as a role in which the man is locked up within the ceremonies of his office:

> And what have kings that privates have not too,
> Save ceremony, save general ceremony?
> And what art thou, thou idol Ceremony?
>
> [4.1.238–40]

Knowing that he is an actor makes Hal more effective than other actors, like the Prince of Navarre or Theseus, who refused to accept their histrionic status, and at the same time his ability and determination to choose the appropriate role and play it totally convincingly make him superior to hams like Bottom and Falstaff who choose roles they cannot manage and overplay their parts in such a way as to reveal that they are acts. Good actors, audiences, and plays share, in the Shakespearean view of theater, a balanced mixture of illusion and reality. Theater in all its aspects "is an art / Which does mend Nature, change it rather; but / The art itself is Nature" (*Winter's Tale*, 4.4.95–97).

But if, in Hal, Shakespeare portrays the perfect actor, as if that question were finally settled, at least in the abstract, his success at once raises certain deeper questions about the uses to which acting and theater may be put. Successful acting in the *Henriad* is ambiguous in its effects, leading as often to deceit, betrayal, and cruelty as to positive social and political achievement. Even at its best, theater may have disastrous consequences for individuals and for society, and it is this possibility, which has shadowily been present in the earlier plays, to which Shakespeare turns directly in *Hamlet*, never forgetting but pushing his concern with actors and audiences slightly aside in order to focus on more far-reaching questions about the relationship of plays and theater to the state and society.

4

Catching the Conscience of the King
Politics and Theater in
Hamlet

The actual conditions of playing in the theater were not the only forces affecting plays and the playwright's conception of his role and his art, for once the theater became professional and public, playing openly six days a week to an audience of several thousands in the capital city of the kingdom, it inevitably ceased to be mere entertainment and became, along with the printing press, a primary means of expressing national values and shaping public opinion on political and social issues. This situation forced the playwright to consider, as the poet writing for a small select audience never had to, just what relationship his work bore to a larger political world in which the English nation was passing from a medieval kingdom to a modern state, a "period of transition," as Marx put it, when "absolute monarchy appeared" because "the old feudal classes were decaying and the medieval burgher class was evolving into the modern bourgeois class, without either of the disputing parties being able to settle accounts with the other."[1] Like all

1. "Moralizing Criticism and Critical Morality: A Polemic Against Karl Henzen," quoted in Paul N. Siegel, "Marx, Engels, and the Historical Criticism of Shakespeare," *Shakespeare Jahrbuch* 113 (1977): 124.

great social changes, the transition was enormously complex and contentious, ultimately involving civil war and a king's head, and it found expression in a host of oppositions: king and parliament, aristocracy and gentry, established church and presbytery, hierarchy and individualism, feudalism and democracy, a landed society and a moneyed one, theology and science.

These many complex oppositions have frequently been simplified as a struggle between the court and the city, or the court and the Puritans, and it was in these terms that the public theaters felt most immediately and directly the mighty opposites at work in society. On the whole, the court and the governing aristocracy tended to favor and support the theater. Marion Jones points out that, "the relationship between Elizabeth and the major dramatists of her reign was not one of straightforward Renaissance patronage. Elizabeth founded no Academy, maintained no playwrights as such, commissioned no play of genius."[2]

But the court and the nobility did, nonetheless, help the theater in numerous and important ways. General protection was afforded the players by a social fiction in which great lords designated the playing companies as their retainers, wearing their livery—Leicester's Men or Lord Strange's Men—and thus gave them the defense of a great name and the legal status needed by any group to exist in Elizabethan society. At one point in the 1580s the most notable actors of the realm were gathered into a group called the Queen's Men, and after the accession of James I in 1603, Shakespeare's company became the King's Men, while other distinguished groups took the names of other members of the royal family. While this sign of royal approval did not involve direct financial support, the major companies were substantially rewarded for playing before the court on

---

2. Marion Jones, "The Court and the Dramatists," in *Elizabethan Theater*, Stratford-Upon-Avon Studies 9 (London: Edward Arnold, 1966), p. 170.

various holidays, and they played often at other bastions of the establishment, the Inns of Court, the universities, and the great houses of the kingdom. Again and again when the players were under attack and the theaters in danger of being closed by the London authorities, the Privy Council intervened either openly in favor of the players or, if the political pressure was too strong to be entirely resisted, to find an acceptable compromise.

No doubt the nature of their own public lives made the queen and the aristocrats friendly to the art of good performance, and both Elizabeth and James commented on their status as royal actors in the theater of the court; but the real bond between theater and court was part of what Roy Strong calls "the most profound alliance" that occurred during the sixteenth and seventeenth centuries "between the new art forms of the Renaissance and the concept of the prince."[3] The new absolute monarchs found in humanist art, particularly the theater, a useful method for propagating an image of their power and dynastic glory, providing propaganda for their political and social ideologies, and in general giving luster to what were for the most part rules of doubtful legitimacy. It is no accident that the deposition of the English king was accompanied by the closing of the theaters in 1642, for the interests of crown and theater across Europe were sufficiently close during this period to justify the poet Denham's observation after the Restoration that the fortunes of the two institutions were identical:

They that would have no KING, would have no Play:
The *Laurel* and the *Crown* together went,
Had the same *Foes*, and the same *Banishment*.[4]

---

3. *Splendor at Court, Renaissance Spectacle and the Theater of Power* (Boston: Houghton Mifflin, 1973), p. 19. See also Steven Orgel, *The Illusion of Power: Political Theater in the English Renaissance* (Berkeley: University of California Press, 1975).

4. "The Prologue to His Majesty," *Poetical Works*, ed. T.H. Banks (New Haven, Conn.: Yale University Press, 1928), p. 94.

While the court and the aristocracy supported the players, they also regulated them, and throughout the sixteenth century a variety of statutes tried to limit the number of playing companies and their freedom to move about the realm. Once the companies settled in London, control became easier, and all plays were required to be read and licensed by a court official, the Master of the Revels, before production or printing. The power was absolute, and players and playwrights were fined and imprisoned for defying the censor, but the Office of the Master of the Revels does not seem to have censored the plays in any very subtle fashion, looking primarily for open attacks on the crown and its policies, satiric treatment of important people, swearing (after 1606 when a prohibition against swearing on the stage was passed), and, above all else, comment on that most sensitive of subjects, religion.[5] No matter how crude and imperfect censorship may have been, it still served as a constant reminder to the public theater of its deep involvement with the vital social and political issues of the day, and to the playwrights that their work was in the public domain in the fullest sense and that they always wrote at their peril.

The foes of both court and theater were most immediately and "dramatically" the Puritans, Puritan intellectuals who never tired of thundering that "all Plaies, as carnall, be obscene and ridiculous,"[6] and Puritan businessmen and aldermen in London who constantly sought to close the theaters because they spread the plague, encouraged idleness, generated riots, presented lewdness on stage, offered convenient places for harlots and pickpockets to work, and in general undermined the commonwealth. The confrontation of the theater with Puritan preacher and civic

5. The most complete discussion of censorship and its effect on the playwrights is to be found in Bentley, *The Professional Dramatist*, chap. 7, "Regulation and Censorship."

6. John Rainolde, *Six Conclusions Touching the Holie Scripture* (1584), quoted in Russell Fraser, *The War Against Poetry* (Princeton, N.J.: Princeton University Press, 1970), p. 9.

authority is staged in Ben Jonson's *Bartholomew Fair* (1614), where the magistrate, Justice Overdo, and the fanatic Puritan, Zeal-of-the-Land Busy, denounce a puppet show for all of the usual reasons, that playing is no "lawful calling," that it is profane, that "the male, among you, putteth on the apparel of the female," and that the theater is an "enormity" which disturbs the peace and cheats the public.

Beneath these specific charges against the "abomination" of playing—which Jonson refutes more easily in his play than the players were able to do in fact—there was in Puritan polemics a more "fundamental antipathy to that dramatic view of life and dramatic kind of art," an "aversion from multiplicity, variety, and sensuous attractiveness," an "excluding mentality."[7] The Puritan mind sought an abstract truth which was not embedded in the sensuous substance of things, and therefore found the world in general and plays in particular to be only the shows of appearance, mere idols and golden calves, the shadows of shadows in Platonic terms. There is considerable irony in the theater's relationship to the Puritans, for while the theater was antithetical by its very nature to Puritan interests and ways of thinking, it was at the same time, in some of its aspects, very much a part of the new and coming world of which Puritanism was the religious manifestation. It was organized financially in an entrepreneurial and capitalistic manner, it played to a democratic audience, and it was popular in appeal.

In the midst of turbulent political and social conflict, the playwrights, understandably, tried to maintain a politically neutral position, and the standard, oft-repeated explanation they offered of the theater's relationship to society was essentially that plays were either mere entertainment or truly moral if understood correctly. They did not portray vice in

7. Patrick Crutwell, *The Shakespearean Moment*, chap. 5, "Puritanism and the Dramatic Attitude," pp. 138, 151, 143. The full history and the meaning of "The Antitheatrical Prejudice" is brilliantly presented in an article with that title by Jonas Barish, *Critical Quarterly* 8 (1966): 329–48.

ways that encouraged it, as was often charged, but rather, as *Hamlet* sums up the tradition of moral apology, held "the mirror up to nature" in order "to show virtue her own feature, scorn her own image, and the very age and body of the time his form and pressure."

But it is clear that the theater was much more deeply involved in political issues than the playwrights admitted, and on the surface at least, the plays of the period seem to have supported the court, which was the social ally of the theater, and championed the old order with which the players had a long association and natural affinities. As Crutwell says, the theater "sprang from, and for its appreciation demanded, a hierarchical view of society. Its tragedy is that of 'noble' personalities, its comedy that of men who will not understand and remain within their social limits, like Malvolio and Sir Epicure Mammon."[8] Ben Jonson's plays are primarily satiric attacks on the major types of new men—the capitalist, the Puritan, the "projector," the scientist (alchemists), the rising entrepreneur, the Machiavellian politician—and Shakespeare's villains, Claudius, Iago, Edmund, or Octavius, are all individualistic self-seekers, rationalists, skeptics, and new-style men of practical affairs. The killing of kings, a frequent theatrical subject, and the attack on authority of any kind are regularly shown in Shakespeare's and other plays of the time to have the most disastrous consequences for individuals and for the kingdom.

But the better plays were never finally homilies on obedience, and looking back from the present it is possible to see many of the greatest plays as covertly, and sometimes openly, revolutionary in effect if not in intent. Christopher Marlowe's great soldiers, scheming merchants, and all-daring philosophers come to bad ends, but the willingness of a Tamburlaine or Faustus to overstep all traditional boundaries in seeking to implement their will to power dominates

8. *The Shakespearean Moment*, p. 151.

their plays and points to the future rather than the past. Shakespeare's king-killers, like Bolingbroke or Macbeth, may bring great sufferings on themselves and on their people, but their rebellions are presented as political and even psychological inevitabilities, and they ultimately achieve tragic stature.

Taken individually, the plays are conservative on the surface—the censor would surely not have licensed them otherwise—but looked at over the long run, from the 1580s to 1642, the theater presents a continuous, increasing series of challenges to traditional authority, to king, father, church, law, family, "nature," and state. These rebellions regularly come to a bad end, and so may be taken as object lessons in the necessity of traditional morality and obedience to the established order, but they are nonetheless the staple of the theater, the subject of most interest to playwrights and audiences. In the hands of later dramatists such as Webster and Ford, rebellion often takes bizarre and openly sensational form—incest, torture, cunning poisonings—and authority becomes hopelessly corrupt or offers only pitiful defenses against its final destruction. No doubt the "Puritans," to use that generic term for so complex a social movement, would have been horrified to think that their own zeal for righteousness, hard work, and responsibility for their own souls before God could be found in the rebellious heroes of the English Renaissance theater, but those figures do express in an exaggerated, though not ultimately untruthful way the absolute desires for freedom and truth which motivated the men who were destroying the old medieval society in order to create the modern world. And just as the playwrights saw and understood the fierce destructive energy which motivated the new men, so they also saw and portrayed on stage the weakness of the old order and its inevitable destruction.

Because Shakespeare was a poet, a writer of fictions, it is not generally recognized that he was also a great historian, the greatest in England until Hobbes, Clarendon, Hume, and

Gibbon. To this day, even, few can match him for the vividness, and perhaps even the accuracy, with which he portrays the motives and cues for passion which lie behind certain basic political stances: the unbending pride in self and contempt for the weakness of others of a man on horseback like Coriolanus, the inability of a legitimist like Richard II to comprehend that the social order which supports him is not eternal and immutable, the political innocence of an idealistic upper-class revolutionary like Brutus, the icy efficiency of the successful prince like Octavius Caesar, and the utter cynicism about all matters of state of a cynic like Falstaff.

Few historians, too, can match Shakespeare for the power with which he portrays certain familiar scenes of political life: Richard III carefully staging the occasion on which the citizens of London petition him to take the crown; Claudius's cool and efficient control of the many tricky affairs of state in his presence chamber in the second scene of *Hamlet;* Octavius and Antony negotiating at the council table the bargain which divides the world between them; Bolingbroke's "Moscow-trial" contrivance of Richard's confession of his failures and resignation of the crown; the futile debate about the return of Helen to the Greeks in Priam's Trojan palace; Julius Caesar's management of his public image in the state procession at the Lupercal and before the Roman crowd shouting for him to be king in the theater.[9]

Shakespeare's concern with history is as broad as it is deep, and nineteen of his thirty-eight plays deal directly and centrally with historical and dynastic matters. In the remaining half, primarily the comedies and romances, political

9. Anne Righter, *Shakespeare and the Idea of the Play* (London: Chatto and Windus, 1962), in her chapter "The Player King," shows the regularity with which Shakespeare associates kings and theater and notes that "Shakespeare's concern with the Player King. . .seems to represent a use of the play metaphor that is almost unique with him. The entire range of English Renaissance drama. . .yields surprisingly little in the way of similar imagery. . ." (p. 135).

questions of rule and authority are always prominent if not central: Othello is the governor of Cyprus, the question of how a state should be ruled is the issue in *Measure for Measure*, the nature of law is basic to *The Merchant of Venice*, and a deposed duke and his tyrannous brother are key figures in the structure of even so light a comedy as *As You Like It*.

On the surface, Shakespeare seems to have used the theater as a political instrument to celebrate England's greatness and the courage of its old heroes, such as brave Talbot or Henry V, teach the history of the nation to its people, and instruct them in the conservative Elizabethan social and political ideology. But below the orthodox and conservative surfaces of his plays Shakespeare constructed a considerably more radical image of the history of his times. Viewed as a whole, his plays present a continuing historical procession in which an old order, a world of community still largely medieval, hierarchical, and humanistic, is always passing on. Its kings are terribly vulnerable like Richard II, Old Hamlet, or Duncan; its knights die like the French chivalry at Agincourt, or like Hotspur, Antony, and Coriolanus at the hands of more efficient powers; its ancient ceremonies of trial-by-combat, duel, coronation, ritual feast, and regal procession fail in Elsinore, Rome, and Westminster; its gods do not respond to confident invocations or to agonized prayers spoken in extremity; its assumed identity with a humanized nature and a morally ordered cosmos disappears on Lear's heath and in Richard's dungeon in Pomfret Castle.

Perhaps the summary image of the passing of this older world comes in *Lear*, where the king, the loyal peer, the band of knights, the court fool, the honest servant, and the representative of all the poor and dispossessed people of the land, Tom O'Bedlam, are driven out of the castle to face the dreadful forces of an indifferent nature on the heath, and sink at last into despair and death on an apocalyptic battlefield. The passing of this older world is always treated by the conservative Shakespeare as a disaster for society and individuals, but it is always the sadly inevitable direction of events.

The direct practical involvement of the players with the court and the city, and the relationship of the plays to the major political and social issues of the time, combine to make it clear that a public theater is inevitably a political theater with a direct bearing on public opinion. In these circumstances a playwright trying to understand his own dramatic art would find it crucial to establish the function of his plays in society and their relation to the welfare of the kingdom. Theory never advanced much beyond the argument that plays improved public morals by making vice ugly and virtue attractive, though the plays themselves commented on political and social issues in complex and sophisticated ways. But in *Hamlet*, written about 1601, Shakespeare undertook a unique examination of the function of the dramatic poet and of theater in the political life of a kingdom.

It is a measure of Shakespeare's belief in the importance of theater, despite the generally low opinion in which it was held in his time, that he makes it one of the central social institutions dealt with in *Hamlet*. The play explores many of the crucial institutions through which Renaissance society expressed its values, kingship and the state, honor and war, love and friendship, education and philosophy, and as it moves from the court of guard on the battlements, through the throneroom, to the bedroom, the chapel, and the graveyard, it comes, seemingly inevitably, to the theater. The setting is ideal for testing the social value of theater, for a play is presented in the royal court, the very center of the kindom's political and moral life, before an audience consisting of the king, the queen, the prince of the realm, the chief councillor, and members of the nobility associated with the court. The tasks set for the play produced in the court of Denmark are of no less importance than the setting and the audience: to reveal a foul crime hidden beneath the glittering surface of the court, to aid a prince of the blood in achieving his revenge, and finally to purge the kingdom of its sickness and restore it to health. In keeping with the setting and the high purpose, the players who perform the internal play in *Hamlet* are not the usual amateurs but a skillful and thoroughly competent professional company, much like Shakespeare's own group, on tour from their theater in Wittenberg.

In his earlier plays Shakespeare regularly set up images of crude and amateurish theaters aiming at little higher goals than pleasure and profit. But in *Hamlet* the situation seems to be ideal, a courtly setting and audience, expert players, a clear and noble conception of the theater, and an epic task. There is no trifling here with petty questions about such matters as the male actors wearing female clothing, but a clear and direct test, with no excuses offered, of whether theater can fulfill the social functions which truly justify it. The test begins with the entrance of the players whom Hamlet had seen and liked so well when he was a student at Wittenberg that with only a little difficulty he can remember and recite lines from one of their old plays,

> The rugged Pyrrhus, he whose sable arms,
> Black as his purpose, did the night resemble
> When he lay couchèd in th' ominous horse,
> Hath now this dread and black complexion smeared
> With heraldry more dismal. Head to foot
> Now is he total gules, horridly tricked
> With blood of fathers, mothers, daughters, sons,
> Baked and impasted with the parching streets,
> That lend a tyrannous and a damned light
> To their lord's murder. Roasted in wrath and fire,
> And thus o'ersizèd with coagulate gore,
> With eyes like carbuncles, the hellish Pyrrhus
> Old grandsire Priam seeks.

[2.2.459–71]

At this point he gives over to the leading player, who goes on to deliver the rest of the lines describing the pitiful death of Priam at the hands of Pyrrhus, the burning of Troy, and the sorrow of Hecuba:

> Anon he finds him,
> Striking too short at Greeks. His antique sword,
> Rebellious to his arm, lies where it falls,
> Repugnant to command. Unequal matched,
> Pyrrhus at Priam drives, in rage strikes wide,
> But with the whiff and wind of his fell sword
> Th' unnervèd father falls.
>
> [2.2.475–81]

These highly rhetorical but very moving[10] lines seem to provide at first sight an imaginative contrast to the events in Elsinore. In both Troy and Elsinore a great king was killed, a queen survived, and a kingdom was destroyed. But reality, if we take Elsinore for reality, falls sadly short of the idealized, imaginative play-world which shows the features of virtue. In place of the scene of heroic death and epic sorrow in Troy, Elsinore offers a secret murder by poison, concealment of the crime, and the hasty remarriage of the queen, who scarcely remembers the old king, to the murderer. Where in the play nature itself sympathizes with the human disaster—"Then senseless Ilium, / Seeming to feel this blow, with flaming top / Stoops to his base"—here in Elsinore the world goes calmly about its business, and both man and nature seem unaware of the dreadful crime or the great change in the kingdom.

Furthermore, the play offers an image of a heroic

---

10. The quality of the verse and its effect on the characters in *Hamlet* is helpfully analyzed in Harry Levin, *The Question of Hamlet* (New York: Oxford University Press, 1959), "An Explication of the Player's Speech," pp. 137–64. The old-fashioned style of the plays-within-the-play is traced to its sources and defended by Carol Replogle, "Not Parody, Not Burlesque: The Play Within the Play in *Hamlet*," *MP* 67 (1969): 150–59.

revenger—which may have been why Hamlet thought of it in the first place—for in the lines that Hamlet delivers, Pyrrhus is avenging the death of his father Achilles in the war at Troy in the heroic style and direct way that Hamlet seems to find so impossible to effect in Elsinore. "The Death of Priam" seems, then, at least at first glance, to present life in idealized terms, showing us in a straightforward way how great kings and queens and noble revengers face their tragic fates with force and courage.

But even as we look, the meaning of the play clouds over. Pyrrhus is the ideal revenger who would be approved by warriors like Achilles and Old Hamlet, and as such he is the model of what Hamlet so often feels he ought to be and what the Ghost urges him to be. But at the same time, Pyrrhus is an image of such terror that he is a living argument against revenge. To put it in another way, Pyrrhus in killing the old king is simultaneously the model of the heroic revenger Hamlet feels he ought to be and a warning against being that revenger. Moreover, if Priam is an image of Old Hamlet, then Pyrrhus is, in one aspect, an image of Claudius murdering the old king. The mirror that "The Death of Priam" holds up to nature shows virtue its own feature in a most ambiguous way, mixing it inextricably with the image of scorn. The players may "tell all," but they do so in a most complex, ironic manner, mixing negative and positive in such a way as to complicate greatly the traditional argument that the theater teaches morality and truth.

The reaction of the audience to "The Death of Priam" is as complex and unsatisfactory as the image the play presents. Polonius—"He's for a jig or a tale of bawdry, or he sleeps"—finds the speech too long and is impressed only by the ability of the actor to shed real tears, and by certain striking words, "That's good. 'Mobled queen' is good." The chief spectator, Hamlet, does not miss the parallels of the play with his own situation in Elsinore—"I, the son of a dear father murdered, Prompted to my revenge by heaven and hell"—but he does seem to take the play in a most literal way, missing all its complexity. He responds to the play, both its content and the counterfeited passion of the player, by a furious denunciation of Claudius and a plan to carry out his revenge. This is an appropriate response to the pitiful death of old Priam and the revenge of Pyrrhus, but it does not seem to take into account the warnings against revenge contained in the play as well. But perhaps it does, for instead of sweeping at once to his revenge, Hamlet delays again and plans another play which will give him, he hopes, more positive evidence that the Ghost's word that Claudius is a murderer by showing him his crime directly before the entire court.·

The kind of ambiguity that characterizes "The Death of Priam" is equally noticeable in that seemingly most effective of all moral plays, "The Mousetrap" or *The Murder of Gonzago*, which Hamlet has the players perform, with the insertion of "a speech of some dozen or sixteen lines" of his own, to catch the conscience of the king. Never, even in theory, has the stage had more powerful effect on guilty creatures sitting at a play than here, where after a dumb show, a number of lines of dialogue between the Player King and Player Queen about the difficulty of maintaining human purpose in time, and a brief scene of a murder in a garden, Claudius is stricken, rises from his seat and calls for light, making it perfectly clear to Hamlet and Horatio that he did indeed murder Old Hamlet in the manner depicted in the play.[11] Murder *will* out and plays can, as Hamlet believes,

11. This straightforward interpretation of events seems to me correct, but there are, as everyone recognizes, extraordinary difficulties of interpretation in the scene, particularly with Caludius's reactions, the dumb show, Gertrude's silence, and Hamlet's constant interference. However, the many different critical interpretations of the scene, ranging from the view that Claudius never committed the crime in the first place to the belief that he did but fails to connect the events of the play with his own actions and takes alarm only at Hamlet's threatening words, all point in the direction of my argument that Shakespeare is showing plays to be ambiguous in meaning and in effect. For an excellent recent summary of the varieties of interpretation of the scene, see, W.W. Robson, "Did the King See the Dumb Show?" *Cambridge Quarterly* 6 (1975): 303–26.

hold the mirror up to nature, not merely reflecting appearances but revealing hidden crimes and making kings fear to be tyrants.

But again the meaning of the play is uncertain, for the murder of Player King is said by Hamlet to be "one Lucianus, *nephew* of the King." With the knowledge of this fact, the play may be taken as either a dramatization of the way in which Claudius the brother killed Old Hamlet, or as a threat of Hamlet the nephew to take revenge on his uncle, or both at once, which would make it simultaneously an exhortation to and a warning against murder. Whatever the extent of the ambiguity, and both meanings seem to be operative, the consequences are again not all that could be ideally desired:

> Shakespeare followed his contemporaries in asserting that a play is an image of truth, but he also was aware that knowledge of the right does not necessarily lead a person to righteousness. Though Claudius, tented to the quick, withdraws in perturbation from "The Murder of Gonzago" and admits to himself that his offense is rank and smells to Heaven, he is Claudius still, his thoughts remain below, and instead of confessing his crime he sets about devising another murder.[12]

Gertrude seems entirely oblivious of the application of *The Murder of Gonzago* to events in Elsinore, and Hamlet is in a totally different way an equally unsatisfactory audience. Throughout the performance of the play he talks to the other spectators, interprets the play for them, criticizes the actors, and generally interferes with the players' attempts to create the illusion of reality. When the play is finished, Hamlet knows for certain that his uncle is the murderer of his father, but instead of sweeping to his revenge, he fails to kill

12. William A. Ringler, Jr., "Hamlet's Defense of the Players," in *Essays on Shakespeare and Elizabethan Drama in Honor of Hardin Craig*, ed. Richard Holsey (Columbia: University of Missouri Press, 1962), p. 211.

Claudius in the chapel, and the best he can manage is a stormy scene in the bedroom with his mother and a mistaken stabbing of old Polonius, after which he tamely allows himself to be shipped off to England.

If Shakespeare set out to assert, or to test, the belief that a play could reveal truth and affect the welfare of kingdoms, that belief founders, like so many other beliefs, in the twisting corridors of Elsinore. The internal plays in *Hamlet* hold a very ambiguous mirror up to nature, and they do not finally have any very immediate effect on the world. And yet they still tell truths, but truths so qualified and so complex, like *Hamlet* itself, that they cannot provide the basis for direct action or any simple moral beliefs. In fact, the central truth which *The Murder of Gonzago* offers is apparently noticed by no one in its audience. The major portion of the internal play consists of a long central section—usually cut in performance—which begins with the Player Queen protesting at great length and with great feeling that she will never marry again should the Player King die. His voice in reply comes from somewhere near the absolute center of playing—an actor in a play playing an actor king talking about life as a series of changing roles—and tells her and the audience that life itself is finally like a play, that men must act out the roles they are given, that like actors we change as circumstances change, and that life is finally swept on in a plot beyond the control of any player in it:

> Our wills and fates do so contrary run
> That our devices still are overthrown;
> Our thoughts are ours, their ends none of our own.
>
> [3.2.215–17]

The Player King and the Player Queen bear obvious resemblances to Old Hamlet and Gertrude, but the Player King does not tell his audience some particular truth about the situation in Elsinore, nor does he counsel some particular

course of action. Instead, he draws the more general conclusion that life is long, that men do not control it, and that
during the course of it they change and play many different
parts. If the Player King is the essential voice of the theater,
as seems to be the case, then the theater is here speaking
directly to the audience about its own nature and telling us
that the real truth a play offers is to be found not in its
content but in its form, in what Leslie Fiedler calls "the myth
of the Cosmic Drama. 'All the world's a stage, . . . the men
and women merely players;' 'struts and frets his hour upon
the stage and then is heard no more.' "[13]

The play-within-the-play is so contrived, Fiedler points
out, that it forces us to accept the myth of the Cosmic Drama
by creating an infinity of theaters, descending in a vortex to
include ever smaller plays within other plays, and expanding
outwards until "Shakespeare in turn is Hamlet to some more
ultimate Shakespeare, in whose reworking of a recalcitrant
matter, we as onlookers are, according to our guilt, Ophelia
or Gertrude, Polonius or the usurping King, walking shadows, poor players."[14] *Hamlet* universalizes this conception of
character as role and the world as a stage which is focused
in the play-within-the-play by showing all of life in Elsinore
as acting and playing, and flooding the play's language with
such words as *act, shape, play, perform, stage, counterfeit,
paint, shadow, mirror, plot, show, part, put on, trappings, motive,
cue, prologue, audience,* and *scene.*[15] When Hamlet in the
midst of the duel scene refuses a drink from the poisoned
cup saying, "I'll play this bout first," or when he tells
Rosencrantz and Guildenstern that they cannot "play" upon

13. "The Defense of the Illusion," p. 92.
14. *Ibid.,* p. 89.
15. The use of the stage imagery and its extent is fully discussed in
Maynard Mack, "The World of Hamlet," *Yale Review* 41 (1952): 502–23,
to which this chapter and the general conception of the self-conscious
playwright are thankfully indebted. For a close examination of all aspects
of theatrical imagery in *Hamlet,* see also Charles R. Forker,
"Shakespeare's Theatrical Symbolism and Its Function in *Hamlet," SQ* 14
(1961): 215–30.

him like a pipe and sound his mystery, the references to the theater are clear. They are still present, though not so obvious, when Polonius instructs his son Laertes on the proper way to live, as if he were an actor learning a part, "And these few precepts in thy memory / Look thou character," or when Hamlet orders his mother not to go to his uncle's bed but to "Assume a virtue, if you have it not."

Once we begin looking at *Hamlet* in this fashion, it soon becomes apparent that it contains few scenes that are not slightly disguised forms of a play-within-a-play. When Rosencrantz and Guildenstern greet Hamlet after their arrival in Elsinore, they pretend that they are merely old friends concerned about his moodiness and melancholy, when in fact they are spies sent by Claudius to find out what is troubling Hamlet and whether he is dangerous. When Polonius sends a messenger to his son in Paris, he advises the man to engage others in conversation and pretend that he does not know Laertes in order to get truthful answers to questions about Laertes's morals. When Claudius and Polonius wish to find out whether Hamlet's madness results from disappointed love, they inevitably stage a little play in which Ophelia pretends to pray in order to draw Hamlet out, while Claudius and Polonius stand like directors and audience behind the arras. Whenever Claudius appears, in fact, he is playing a part. He is a murderer, a regicide, and an adulterer, but he continually plays the part of a wise and efficient king, acting always for the good of his kingdom and urging the members of his family and his court to follow sensible courses of action.

From time to time this submerged or latent theater in *Hamlet* becomes almost overt. It is close to the surface in Hamlet's pretense of madness, the "antic disposition" he puts on to protect himself and prevent his antagonists from plucking out the heart of his mystery. It is even closer to the surface when Hamlet enters his mother's room and holds up, side by side, the pictures of the two kings, Old Hamlet and Claudius, and proceeds to describe for her the true nature of the choice she has made, presenting truth by means of a show. Similarly, when he leaps into the open grave at Ophelia's funeral, ranting in high heroic terms, he is acting out for Laertes, and perhaps for himself as well, the folly of excessive, melodramatic expressions of grief.

The concluding scene of the play, the duel between Laertes and Hamlet, is another elaborately staged play-within-the-play. The duel is a play in the sense of an exercise or game of skill; it is also a play in the sense that each of the major characters on stage is an actor playing a role. The king is pretending to be a beneficent ruler and a concerned but loyal stepfather, who is sponsoring the exercise of warlike and manly skills within his court; Hamlet is pretending to be simply a duelist, with no misgivings whatsoever about the dangers lurking in the situation; and Laertes is playing the part of the honest sportsman out for a little exercise and pleased with an opportunity to display his skill with the rapier. The queen and the courtiers, gathered around watching the duel, form an audience, and are identified by Hamlet—"You . . . that are but mutes or audience to this act"—in such a way as to suggest that this audience, like so many others in Shakespeare's plays, looks on but never really understands very much.

So totally does reality take on the form of theater in *Hamlet* that the world itself becomes the outside walls of a theater, "this goodly frame, the earth"—"frame" being the technical term for the outer structure of the theater—and the heavens themselves are finally no more real than the painted underside of the cover or "shadow" extending out over the stage, "this majestical roof fretted with golden fire." Within this world the most fundamental values and actions are revealed as being essentially theatrical. As Hamlet watches Fortinbras's brave army on the way to Poland to fight for a plot of ground not large enough to bury all the men who will be slain in battle for it, his remarks reveal that he fully understands that the struggle—"even for an eggshell"—has neither sufficient causes nor sufficient rewards to justify it in any realistic sense. Instead, it is a brave and desperate enterprise staged to provide a scene in which honor can be realized:

> Rightly to be great
> Is not to stir without great argument,
> But greatly to find quarrel in a straw
> When honor's at the stake.
>
> [4.4.53–56]

Reality will not support man's dreams, and man must therefore contrive situations, such as the Polish adventure, to play out and realize his dream of honor.

Shakespeare's awareness of the universality of playing goes even deeper, however, goes to the very root of things. At the beginning of act 5, Hamlet, returned from his sea voyage, stands in the graveyard looking at Yorick's skull and ponders the meaning of death. All mankind, he realizes, must come to this state. The lady with her fine clothes and cosmetics, the lawyer with all his skills and learning, the landowner with his deeds and charters, the conquerors of the world like Caesar and Alexander must end, Hamlet now realizes, as a heap of bones and a handful of dust. If this is the reality from which we come and to which we return, then how can man regard that portion of existence we call life as any more than a part, be it that of a king or beggar, played by an actor on the changing stage of the world? Even death does not remove one from the world's stage: "Let four captains," says Fortinbras giving funeral directions for the Danish prince, "bear Hamlet like a soldier to the stage."

There are two quite different conceptions of theater's effect upon the world at work throughout *Hamlet*. The first is a conventional moral view, very similar to that found in Sidney's *Apology*, which argues that plays can directly influence the moral and political life of kingdoms by presenting idealized images of the world—Priam's Troy or Gonzago's Vienna—that throw light on the world in which

they are presented and effect change by catching the con-
sciences of kings. In Sidney's words, which come very close
to the situation and the imagery of *Hamlet*, tragedy "openeth
the greatest wounds, and sheweth forth the Ulcers that are
covered with Tissue; . . . maketh Kinges feare to be Tyrants,
and Tyrants manifest their tirranicall humours."[16] This is
Hamlet's view precisely, and his idea of a theater has much
in common with Sidney's views. Like Sidney, he dislikes the
"bawdry" of the clowns and the ranting style of "robustious
periwig-pated" tragedians who "tear a passion to tatters, to
very rags, to split the ears of the groundlings, who for the
most part are capable of nothing but inexplicable dumb
shows and noise" (3.2.9–12). Hamlet worries, too, about the
clowns who can destroy plays by speaking "more than is set
down for them." His preference is for carefully structured
plays "well digested in the scenes," and for a corresponding
"temperance that may give it smoothness" in both the acting
style and the language of the plays. His view of the "purpose
of playing, whose end, both at the first and now, was and is,
to hold, as t'were, the mirror up to nature; to show virtue her
own feature, scorn her own image, and the very age and
body of the time his form and pressure" (3.2.20–24), is a
precise statement of the Sidnean conception of a morally
effective theater.

Leslie Fiedler remarks on the similarity of Hamlet who
emends *The Murder of Gonzago* to Shakespeare who transformed the *ur-Hamlet* into *Hamlet*, and Robert Nelson states
flatly that "Hamlet's 'idea of a theater' constitutes a
Shakespearean *art poètique* in miniature,"[17] but the play does
not finally support this identification. Hamlet is the spokes-

---

16. *Apology for Poetry*, p. 177. The example which Sidney offers here to
support his claim for theater comes from Plutarch's "Life of Pelopidas,"
in which a king is reformed by seeing Euripides' *Troades* dealing with the
sorrows of Hecuba, also the subject of the lines Hamlet asks the players
to recite on their appearance in Elsinore. For a detailed discussion of this
matter, see William A. Ringler, Jr., "Hamlet's Defense of the Players," pp.
201–11.

17. *Play Within A Play*, p. 28.

man for a Renaissance ideal conception of the social effect of theater,[18] as he is the spokesman for so many other Renaissance ideals which die in Elsinore. The Player King is the spokesman for a very different conception of theater which had been emerging in Shakespeare's earlier plays and now finds full expression in *Hamlet*.

The Player King tells us that the dramatic mode itself, prior to any particular characters, scenes, or actions which may body it forth, is not some kind of artistic contrivance for rearranging the world in order to reveal hidden truths and to shape events, but is itself a most realistic representation of the human condition, a true way of imaging life. What man seems to be at one moment, he is not the next, and the human condition may therefore be correctly represented as that of an actor playing a part. Man's life is never entirely within his own control, and he is thus properly figured as an actor who appears to be controlling his own destiny, while in fact he is only moving through some inescapable order of events laid down by a distant invisible author. It is not the contents of a play (the subject matter) but the theatrical mode itself that finally serves "to hold the mirror up to nature—to show virtue her own feature, scorn her own image, and the very age and body of the time his form and pressure." What it shows, however, is not some certain truth, some clear moral which can be taken home by the audience—if only they ever really heard all there was to hear—but a condition of life like the theater itself, ambiguous, changing, transient. This is not, of course, a new

18. The case for the views of acting and playing being the aristocratic Hamlet's, not the professional playwright Shakespeare's, is ably argued by Roy Battenhouse, "The Significance of Hamlet's Advice to the Players," in *The Drama of the Renaissance*, ed. Elmer M. Blistein (Providence: Brown University Press, 1970). Battenhouse believes that Hamlet's views on playing are another instance of his disastrously wrongheaded idealism, while it seems to me that they are better understood as a clear statement of a traditional view of the nature and value of theater which is to be tested during the course of the play and found not altogether wrong but inadequate.

idea but a very sophisticated and powerfully applied version of the old trope that man is only an actor in a brief play on the stage of the world,[19] and it is not presented directly but woven into the substance and the plot.

The plot of the play, in one of its many aspects, carries Hamlet from his Renaissance view of the power of art to change the world to an acceptance of the view, at once very ancient and very modern, that art, particularly the art of theater, reveals to man not his power over the world but his own unreal status and relative helplessness within it. As a student at Wittenberg—a university seems the proper setting for ideals—Hamlet was a regular playgoer, and though he disliked many of the realities of the public theater—the "groundlings," the clowns, the jigs and bawdry, the inexplicable dumbshows, the ranting style of some players—he nonetheless held a high opinion of what plays could ideally be and do, and he formed friendships with the actors of at least one company. But on his return to Elsinore, where playing is the only way of life, he begins an education in the many different forms that theater can take and the many different functions it can perform. Here a murderer pretends to be a benevolent king, a fool pretends to be a wise councillor, a lustful and adulterous woman pretends to be a faithful queen and mother. Ophelia is cast for the part of Juliet, but in the test is revealed as only a timid daughter tamely obeying a foolish father; Rosencrantz and Guildenstern play the childhood friends and college chums, but are in actuality self-seeking toadies of the king. Elsinore is a play contrived to cover up many crimes, including the central crime of regicide, and Hamlet responds to his discovery of this fact by becoming at first suspicious of all

---

19. The earlier forms of this traditional topos are dealt with by E.R. Curtius, *European Literature and the Latin Middle Ages*, trans. Willard Trask, Bollingen Series 36 (New York: Pantheon, 1953), pp. 138–44. The central statement of the image in the Renaissance is probably that of Erasmus in *The Praise of Folly;* while its development in the drama is summarized by Anne Righter, *Shakespeare and the Idea of the Play.*

forms of acting. When his mother asks him why the death of his father "seems . . . so particular with thee?" his response reveals how deeply he dislikes all theatrical arts:

> Seems, madam? Nay, it is. I know not "seems."
> 'Tis not alone my inky cloak, good mother,
> Nor customary suits of solemn black,
> Nor windy suspiration of forced breath,
> No, nor the fruitful river in the eye,
> Nor the dejected havior of the visage,
> Together with all forms, moods, shapes of grief,
> That can denote me truly. These indeed seem,
> For they are actions that a man might play,
> But I have that within which passes show;
> These but the trappings and the suits of woe.
>
> [1.2.76–86]

But he has no alternative to expressing his grief in the prescribed form of sighs and tears and the traditional black costume, and similarly there is no way of acting, in the sense of doing, in Elsinore other than acting in the sense of playing. And so, at first merely in order to protect himself, he takes on the role of a madman; but the role also becomes the means of revealing truth, as well as concealing it, and allows him to contrive scenes in which he exposes Rosencrantz and Guildenstern for the hapless idiots they really are and Polonius as the bumbling fool he actually is. Soon the play becomes larger than the player and reveals Hamlet, unbeknownst to himself, as more than a little mad in his excessive agony over "the thousand natural shocks that flesh is heir to" and his consequent despair of life. The restored confidence in the value of playing which the success of the "antic disposition" encourages, finds full expression in the arrival in Elsinore of the professional players, in Hamlet's exposition of the art and purpose of playing, and in the performance of the two internal plays. From Hamlet's point of view, the players "tell all" and their plays fulfill the highest claims for a noble art in revealing the truth about Elisnore and forcing the king to face his guilt. His own apparent success soon afterwards in forcing his mother to see and acknowledge her own moral failure by using the two pictures to show her just what she has done seems to confirm the ability of theater to reveal truth and change conduct.

But the meaning and the effects on the audience of these internal plays are, as we have seen, extremely ambiguous, and they do not bring about the immediate reformation of the kingdom. Claudius plans to commit another murder by means, characteristically, of another pretense, sending Hamlet to England, supposedly for his safety. Instead of accomplishing his revenge, Hamlet goes obediently off on his sea voyage, along the way pausing to look and reflect upon the spectacle of Fortinbras's army on its way to Poland, which seems to sum up what the play as a whole has shown us to this point about both the power of playing and its futility. The army, in its march toward "imminent death," is simply playing out the role the world has assigned to it, and the game is not worth the candle; but in thus playing its part bravely and with high style it is achieving the honor it seeks, which it can find in no other way.

The ironic conception of theater implicit in the scene of Fortinbras's army on its way to Poland is driven home to Hamlet by his narrow excape from Claudius's plot to have him executed in England, and when he returns to Denmark, he is able to face the fact of death in the graveyard and recognize that all of life is a play in which man is an actor, not the playwright, playing out a part he did not choose in a plot not of his own making. The playwright is unknown, "a divinity that shapes our ends, / Rough-hew them how we will," and the play in which Hamlet is now cast, the duel scene, is larger than he or Claudius, who thinks that he makes and directs it, anticipates, for it requires the death of both.

The Player King tells his unheeding audience that the truth a play reveals is that men are like actors in a play, not like the playwright who makes it, and this is what Hamlet learns. The change he undergoes from a young lord confidently instructing players in their art, pronouncing on the true nature of theater and its ability to catch the conscience of a king, and sitting upon the stage and criticizing the performance, to an actor in a play whose purpose or direction he does not control or even understand, measures the distance that the conception of theater travels in the course of *Hamlet*.

In a way Shakespeare is making enormous claims for the social value of his art in contending that it shows not merely images of the real world or personifications of vices and virtues, but the very structure of life itself prior to any particular form it may take or any particular moral it may illustrate. But at the same time he withdraws from the position of moral propagandist who affects the welfare of the state by making "guilty creatures sitting at a play . . . by the very cunning of the scene . . . struck so to the soul that presently / They have proclaimed their malefactions" (2.2.596–99). Shakespeare was, as Philip Edwards remarks, "in love with an art that was never immune from his own skepticism,"[20] and this skepticism about the theater forced him away from the moralist's position to a more philosophic view.

What all the internal plays of *Hamlet*, not just the formal plays-within-the-play, reveal is that plays can be used to conceal truth as well as reveal it, and that they can be used to manipulate reality for base purposes as well as noble ones. Furthermore, their meaning is usually morally ambiguous; for just as *The Death of Priam* encourages revenge and warns against it at the same time, so the march of the army to Poland is at once a heroic venture and a piece of utter folly. Even when a play reveals a hidden truth, as *The*

20. *The Confines of Art*, p. 15.

Murder of Gonzago does, the audience is not likely to see what is there any more than Gertrude sees the ghost in her bedroom, nor does it ever have much effect on the course of events. One play simply gives way to another play, and the truth of all the plays is ambiguous and provisional. Kings and princes move across the great stage of the world, stealing crowns, revenging the death of fathers, watching plays, and each of the episodes in their violent and bloody lives is merely an event in some unknown plot in which they play the part required of them. Withdraw one step, as *Hamlet* constantly invites us to, and *Hamlet* itself along with all Shakespeare's other political plays become to the world in which Mary Queen of Scots is a double plot to Elizabeth, Essex's followers arrange to have *Richard II* played in the city at the time of his rebellion, and Elizabeth manages her suspenseful production of naming James as her successor only at the climactic moment, what "The Death of Priam" and *The Murder of Gonzago* are to the play-world of *Hamlet*.

5

The Playing Tradition in the Popular Theater

The Morality Play in
King Lear

Sir Philip Sidney greatly disapproved of the Elizabethan public theater, and in his *Apology for Poetry* he provides a vivid description of what performances were like in the early 1580s before the appearance of the great playwrights and actors. Romance provided one of the staple intrigue plots of misadventure, thwarted love, far wanderings, suspense, and happy endings:

> for ordinary it is that two young Princes fall in love. After many traverces, she is got with childe, delivered of a faire boy; he is lost, groweth a man, falls in love, and is ready to get another child; and all this in two hours space. . . .[1]

Romantic plots like this provided the opportunity, on an unlocalized stage with only rudimentary scenery, for imag-

---

1. *Apology for Poetry*, p. 197. Other quotes and most of the details in this paragraph are taken from Sidney.

inary travel to far-flung exotic places: "you shal have *Asia* of the one side, and *Affrick* of the other, and so many other under-kingdoms, that the Player, when he commeth in, must ever begin with telling where he is, or els the tale wil not be conceived." Elaborate machines—a "hidious monster" belching smoke and fire, thrones lowered from above, a flaming "hellmouth," or a boiling cauldron into which the villain drops—provided delightful, though probably somewhat crude, spectacular effects. Rich costumes made up for the lack of scenery. The world of the court and "high-society" were presented, and great dynastic battles, "represented with foure swords and bucklers," were staged, accompanied by fearsome sound effects produced by a thunder machine. Swift changes of setting, from a garden in which ladies walk gathering flowers to a fearful shipwreck, provided variety of scene for all tastes. "Kings and Clownes" mingled easily on this stage, and the popular comic figure—vice, witty servant, or country bumpkin—was freely "thrust in . . . by head and shoulders, to play a part in majesticall matters." The clown's jokes were somewhat greasy, "scurrility, unwoorthy of any chast eares," and the humor was often an "extreame shew of doltishnes" of the pratfall and custard-pie variety, or such rough provincial fun as mockery of foreigners and their mistakes in the English language.

Sidney's description of the theater as it existed in the 1580s reminds us that Shakespeare—whose plays contain instances of all the standard features on which Sidney remarks—and the other Elizabethan dramatists did not invent their theater, as sometimes seems the case, but began work in a popular theater with well-established theatrical traditions of its own. Although the necessary conditions for the great age of Elizabethan theater did not exist until 1576, with the building of the first professional theater and the settling in London of acting companies, the players drew on a tradition extending far into the past to the performance in certain cathedral towns of medieval mystery cycles portraying the biblical pageant of human life from the creation of the world to the Last Judgment. During the fifteenth century small groups of professional players appeared and, over the next century and a half, developed a style of playing and a type of play, romances of the type Sidney describes and morality plays,[2] in performances in great houses and on tour through the towns and countryside.

The repertory and acting styles of these companies were the basis of the standard playing tradition of the English public theaters, and the new professional playwrights, even while modifying and eventually changing the tradition, wrote plays that conformed in many ways to the old patterns. They put kings and clowns on the same stage; allowed for jigs and wrote in clown acts with trained dogs; created characters who were still recognizable as stock popular types of the older theater, the Vice, Herod, the Prodigal Son, and Lady Vanity; provided double and triple plots to satisfy the desire for variety of event and episode; dropped villains in cauldrons, sent sinners down flaming hell-mouths, and staged debates between vice and virtue, Riot and Youth, good and evil angels.

These are, however, only the most obvious signs of a conformity to a popular theatrical tradition which also manifested itself in the plotting and structure of the plays themselves. Shakespeare's conception of the sweep of English history owes much, it has been argued, to the vast panorama of human life in the old mystery cycles,[3] which he could have seen in one of the last performances in Coventry, near Stratford, in his boyhood. Whether he ever actually saw the mystery plays, many of his most powerful scenes seem to

2. The best descriptions of this tradition and its development are to be found in David Bevington, *From "Mankind" to Marlowe* (Cambridge, Mass.: Harvard University Press, 1962); and T.W. Craik, *The Tudor Interlude: Stage, Costume and Acting* (Leicester: Leicester University Press, 1958).

3. For an excellent discussion of the evidence for Shakespeare's familiarity with the mystery cycle plays, see Emrys Jones, *Origins of Shakespeare* (Oxford: Oxford University Press, 1977), chap. 2, "Shakespeare and the Mystery Cycles."

be secular versions of sacred events portrayed in the old cycles. Iago's identification of Othello at the Saggitary bears a marked resemblance to Judas's betrayal of Christ, Lady Macbeth's handwashing to Pilate's, and the death of John of Gaunt to the passing of Abraham. The structural influences of the morality plays with their allegorical figures and set plot patterns are even more pervasive and pronounced. Othello between the good officer Cassio and the evil officer Iago, Lear between his one good daughter and his two evil daughters, Prince Hal between Falstaff and Hotspur, are but three examples among many of the characteristic morality-play placement of Rex or Everyman between Virtue and Vice. The Vice himself is, as Bernard Spivack has shown in careful detail,[4] the ancestor of many of Shakespeare's major villains, particularly of Iago. The plot of *Othello* is only one obvious instance of many Shakespearean plays built on the familiar morality play pattern of temptation, sin, repentance, and salvation, while the *Respublica* plot of "God's Nemesis who finally brings down judgment on the Protestant Vices, Avarice, Insolence, and Oppression, and restores the commonwealth to 'tholde good estate,' "[5] underlies most of the Shakespearean history plays, particularly those dealing with Prince Hal.

The few examples cited above give some idea of the extent to which Shakespeare's plays conformed to the popular playing tradition which dominated his theater, but each of the examples also suggests the ways in which Shakespeare was modifying the tradition even as he worked in it. The moral structure of sin, repentance, and salvation is unmistakeably the basic plot of *Othello*, but the salvation is so problematic that Othello's final speech and suicide may represent either damnation or salvation. Iago may owe his lineaments to the Vice, but his mysterious motivation and his

4. *Shakespeare and the Allegory of Evil* (New York: Columbia University Press, 1958).

5. Howard Felperin, *Shakespearean Representation* (Princeton, N.J.: Princeton University Press, 1977), p. 53.

rigid realism give a psychological dimension to his character not found in any morality-play personification of evil. Hal may be Lusty Juventus, counseled by Vices and Virtues, gradually learning to be the true prince and the savior of the commonwealth, but Vices and Virtues like Falstaff and Hotspur speak with such ambiguous voices that it is difficult to tell which is which, and the "mirror of all Christian kings" is so complex a character, and the nature of rule so mixed a business, that we are left wondering whether the restoration of the kingdom represents a triumph of morality or of Machiavellian politics.

To put the matter in its simplest terms, Shakespeare and the other new playwrights of the time were poised between the traditional patterns which the theater had developed to represent and order life in various formal schemes, and a new experimentalism which led them to imitate life in more realistic ways and follow it wherever it seemed to lead. The weaker dramatists—a Peele or a Dekker, to suggest the range—reduced the tension, which they may never have felt very strongly, by stressing the patterns and limiting the individuality of the characters. The greater dramatists seem to have accepted the tension and made it the very subject of their drama. The gigantic individuals created by the iconoclastic Marlowe struggle to control their own destiny against the pull of Fortune's Wheel, and Doctor Faustus, who tries by magic to make the world take the forms of his mind, is forced to trudge drearily down that ancient path from a bargain with Satan, past devils with firecrackers, into the papier-mâché hell-mouth which was one of the stock properties of his theater.

In Shakespeare, at once more conservative and more daring of mind than Marlowe, the opposition between old structures and the desire to follow nature where it led is at the maximum. His characters are usually masterpieces of psychological realism, and yet they operate very close to such conventional schemes as "murder will out" or the standard romantic plot of comedy which dictates that Jack shall always have Jill. Howard Felperin sums up this conflict between Shakespeare's conception of a new dramatic style and subject matter and the given realities of the theater in which he worked in the following way: "The evidence suggests that Shakespeare, far from being an unwitting medium of theatrical change through whose pen archaism and naturalism flow in proportions varying with the date of a given play, is rather the deliberate mediator of theatrical change, concentrating his archaism at certain strategic points, fully aware of the outmodedness of the forms and figures at his disposal."[6] The "strategic points" at which the archaism is most concentrated are the various plays-within-the-play, which are for the most part written in a distinctly old-fashioned style. "The Pageant of the Nine Worthies," "Pyramus and Thisbe," the tavern play "in King Cambyses' Vein," "The Death of Priam," and *The Murder of Gonzago*, objectify the conventions of the popular theater in which Shakespeare had to work and allow him to ask questions dramatically about their effectiveness and the relationship of this tradition to his own plays.

These same questions are also examined in numerous other scenes which, while not bracketed off from the action as formal plays-within-the-play, have nonetheless all the configurations of morality plays. Indeed, whenever in the midst of Shakespeare's more-or-less realistic plays a scene appears with distinct morality-play characteristics, it takes on, because of the stylistic contrast, the quality of a set-piece or internal play: Richard III's appearance "aloft between two Bishops" with a "book of prayer" in his hand, pretending to be a pious recluse deaf to the pleas of the crowd of citizens below that he accept the crown. This allegorical scene has been carefully contrived by Richard and Buckingham precisely to get the crown, and just beneath its surface the basic elements of a theater are obvious—a prearranged play with a definite purpose, a stage and props, actors, and an audience. The world takes the shape of a

6. *Ibid.*, p. 59.

morality play again in *Richard II*, where Richard's carefully managed descent, with appropriate speeches, from the high walls of Flint Castle, down the steps, to the "base court" below, enacts the fall of princes from high to low degree. As a representative of the old political order, Richard is closely associated with the old style of playing as well, and he sets up another morality play in the deposition scene where the true king and the usurper face one another and debate, each with a hand on the crown between them. After Richard's hand falls and Bolingbroke presumably puts the crown on his head, Richard emblematizes his loss of regal identity and disappearance into oblivion by dashing a mirror on the ground, breaking his image into a thousand pieces.

Despite a common view that Shakespeare worked happily and easily in the theater he inherited, all the internal plays written in the old style, from "The Pageant of the Nine Worthies" to *The Murder of Gonzago*, suggest that he was constantly trying to distance himself as a playwright from the older tradition in order to ask a variety of questions about its effectiveness. The evidence is complex, of course. The examples from *Richard II* suggest, for example, that the morality style can represent Richard's situation truthfully, but that it is politically ineffective, while the scene from *Richard III* suggests that old-style theater can be effective even while it distorts the truth. But whatever the particular mix, there is always something wrong when the archaic style is used, either in the plays-within-the-plays proper or in the scenes which resemble morality plays in all but name.

The nature of Shakespeare's suspicions about the old style can be seen clearly in *Troilus and Cressida*, where he sets up one of his most elaborate theatrical perspectives in the scene in the Greek camp in which Cressida gives Diomedes her love and the favor Troilus had earlier given her. As she acts out her faithlessness, playing the part of Lust or False Faith to Diomedes' Lord Vanity, she is watched, without her knowledge, from the distance by Ulysses and Troilus, and at another remove by Thersites, who is watching Troilus watch Cressida. The purpose of the "play" is deceit of some not quite certain kind, and each of the "audiences" finds a different meaning in it. Ulysses is not particularly moved by what he takes as only another moral instance of the unfaithfulness of a light woman, while the satirist Thersites delightedly revels in the proof that all the world consists of cuckolds and whores. Troilus refuses to believe what he sees and saves his sanity only by concluding that the Cressida he watched cannot be the Cressida he loved—"This is and is not, Cressid"—while we in the last audience of all are left to judge the full realistic complexity of mind of a frightened young girl in a soldiers' camp, who is a coquette by nature, but who did once love Troilus and now blames herself even as she betrays her earlier love. It is possible to treat the scene between Cressida and Diomedes as a morality play, as Ulysses and Thersites with their limited knowledge do, only by ignoring the deeper truth of Cressida and her situation which Shakespeare has provided in his play.

The reductiveness of the morality-play conventions, their inability to reveal the full human truth with which Shakespeare was concerned, is presented even more starkly in *Othello*, where Iago arranges that traditional morality-play device, a dumb-show, in which Othello sees, but for the most part does not hear, Cassio and Iago talking about the whore Bianca's love for Cassio. Deceived by sights such as his handkerchief worked with strawberries, and unenlightened by the poet's words about the true meaning of the scene, Othello construes "Poor Cassio's smiles, gestures, and light behaviors / Quite in the wrong" (4.1.103–04), and assumes that he is watching some simple morality play in which Vice boasts to Virtue of his enjoyment of Lewdness. And so he is, but the form of the presentation allows him to completely misinterpret the parts and, with terrible consequences, to remain ignorant of the extraordinarily complex human reality that lies below the surface of the dumb-show, and, by implication, the theatrical tradition that it here represents.

It is not, I believe, that Shakespeare thoroughly disliked and scorned the old style as other new dramatists like

Jonson and Marlowe did "the jigging veins of rhyming mother wits," but rather that he was always uneasily concerned about his own deep involvement with this theatrical tradition and worried about its ability to realize what he conceived of as being the full potentiality of art in the theater. And in *Lear*, where his indebtedness to the old style and his transcendence of it are both at a maximum, he brings his concerns about the old theatrical tradition to a climax.

Of all Shakespeare's plays, *King Lear* is most obviously structured in the morality-play manner. The king is placed between good and evil daughters, while the duke, whose experiences parallel the king's, is positioned between a legitimate good son and an illegitimate evil one. The plot of the play conflates several standard morality patterns, the education of the prince in the nature of true government, Everyman's discovery of who will go with him into death, and the even more basic temptation pattern of sin, repentance, and salvation. The morality-play elements are so concentrated in the Gloucester subplot with its obvious pattern and its allegorical events such as trial by combat, that one of the characters in the play, Edmund, can even recognize that he is playing in a morality play: "and pat he comes," he says, speaking of the obviously contrived entrance of Edgar at just the right moment, "like the catastrophe in the old comedy."

Subplots in Shakespeare are often a variant form of the play-within-the-play, and the Gloucester plot stands as an internal morality play in *Lear*, treating the same pattern of events in a different mode than the more realistic Lear plot. The contrast of the two plots, one a morality play and the other, while intensely formal, closer to the semirealistic style that Shakespeare himself developed, provides a perfect confrontation of the old and the new theatrical styles. The greater psychological and moral complexities of the Lear plot extend from the motivations of the initial acts which precipitate the plots—Lear's tangled desires for love, obedience, and feedom from further responsibility; and Gloucester's simple carnal sin in begetting Edmund—to their conclusions, in which Gloucester's heart "bursts smilingly" on reunion with his true son, while Lear is left to suffer and ponder the blankness of death on the face of his beloved child. The tendency of the morality-play mode to simplify life and move it toward an instructive if not an entirely happy ending is focused in act 4, in two parallel internal plays of regeneration which children arrange for their fathers in order to restore to them some faith in life.

When Edgar places his old, blind father on some sort of low step, informs him that he is on the edge of Dover Cliff, allows him to assume a heroic stance and jump off, and then picks him up, after he has tumbled a foot or so, to persuade him that he has miraculously survived, the Gloucester plot expresses openly the morality play latent in it from the beginning. And Edgar, who sets up this dramatic demonstration of an abstract idea, contains in himself the attitudes and values which inform the morality play. Until his last words—"speak what we feel, not what we ought to say"—he has exhibited a pronounced tendency toward the conventional, the sententious, the formal and theological understandings of life. Even in his assumed "madness" he explains evil in terms of conventional morality and the devils of folktale.

The point of Edgar's brief morality play is clear. The last sight Gloucester saw was the diabolic face and the hands of a man reaching to tear out his eyes, and he staggered away from this total denial of humankind, away from the heath and toward the sea, despairing of any value in life. He still believes in the existence and power of nameless gods, but because of what he has experienced he can no longer believe in their goodness. Suicide seems his only recourse. He engages his son Edgar, still disguised as a mad beggar, to lead him to the cliff at Dover; but Edgar, who despite all he himself has endured continues to believe in life in a conventional way, arranges an object-lesson to persuade his father that life itself, under any conditions, is a miracle to be valued and cherished so long as we still breathe, have heavy substance, speak, and bleed not. Gloucester learns his lesson

well—though he forgets it soon afterward when new mis-
fortune comes—and he neatly sums up the moral of the little
miracle play:

> henceforth I'll bear
> Affliction till it do cry out itself,
> "Enough, enough," and die.
>
> [4.6.75–77]

No doubt we should applaud Edgar for teaching and
Gloucester for learning such sound doctrine, but *Lear* itself
has already shown us so many scenes of loss and degrada-
tion·that by this point it requires more than saying that life
is a miracle because the heart still beats to make us believe
it. And while Gloucester may be taken in by Edgar's miracle,
the grotesque awkwardness on stage of that "miracle"
emphasizes the fact that it is only a shabby theatrical device,
imposed on a man of less than first-rate intellect to make him
go on living some dream of the gods' unfathomable caring
for human life which is at odds with what has happened and
will happen.[7]

The relevant literary gloss for this scene is a later
morality play, the story of the Grand Inquisitor in *The
Brothers Karamazov*. There, the Grand Inquisitor berates
Christ for leaving the mass of simple mankind, men much
like Gloucester, completely free to choose or not to choose

7. Harry Levin, "The Heights and the Depths: A Scene from *King
Lear*," in *More Talking of Shakespeare*, ed. John Garrett (London: Long-
mans, 1959), shows that Edgar's "miracle" is a reenactment of the descent
from on high which the play as a whole dramatizes. He shows also that
Edgar, whose misery on the heath brought Lear to a sense of fellow-
feeling, is the appropriate instrument for saving Gloucester from despair.
But Levin does not see that the "miracle" is also a dramatization of what
has previously happened and is forced to call it a "pious fraud." He
concludes that staging it would have been "difficult" on Shakespeare's
nonrepresentational stage and "impossible" on a proscenium stage. The
inevitable awkwardness is, it seems to me, a characteristic Shakespearean
exposure of the illusory quality of all theater and, by its very obviousness,
another comment on the difficulty the old-style theater had in creating the
necessary degree of illusion.

God. The great number of men, says the Grand Inquisitor, cannot bear to be without the miraculous; they "would see a sign," and Christ, by his refusal of the devil's temptation to hurl himself down from the temple, or to come down from the cross, has denied them the miracles, the mystery, the authority—in short, the solid proof—that they need in order to endure the hardships of life and continue to believe in a just and caring God. The church has supplied these solid proofs, requiring of man in return only the awful existential freedom that he never wanted anyway. But the Grand Inquisitor, who knows that freedom and certainty are incompatible, regards the miracles his church has engineered as necessary tricks designed to ease the minds of the frightened and block the sight of that fearsome emptiness in which true faith must operate.

Edgar, though lacking the Grand Inquisitor's subtle mind, would seem to be supplying his father with the same kind of miracle that the Inquisitor's church supplied, at the same expense, and for the same reason. But while Edgar's miracle may be a trick, it is a trick devised to stage and state a truth in such a powerful way that Gloucester can understand that truth feelingly, though unable to reason it out for himself. Edgar's morality play is built on two opposing perspectives, looking down and looking up. Edgar, like the poet in the theater, creates both perspectives with words for his blind father. As the two supposedly stand at the edge of the cliff, the imagination is directed downward and yet farther downward. At first the perspective focuses on some birds part way down which "show scarce so gross as beetles"; then it descends halfway to a man clinging to the cliff, a samphire-gatherer who "seems no bigger than his head." Then it plunges to the bottom to fishermen who seem no larger than mice, a ship become as small as her boat, and at last to the surge of the ocean, so far away it cannot be heard as it "on th' unnumb'red idle pebble chafes," rolling backward and forward endlessly. We have moved by means of details, each of which shows life in diminished form, to the point where life vanishes into a sea of meaningless movement.

This precipitous movement parallels and summarizes the experiences of Lear and Gloucester and Edgar up to this point in the play. They too have begun on high, certain of their own power and titles, assured of the value of human life, and trusting in the goodness and richness of the world. But as the play proceeds, the world narrows from a spacious kingdom of "champains rich'd / With plenteous rivers and wide-skirted meads" to the storm-tortured heath. And as the world constricts, man diminishes in size and importance from king and father to "the thing itself . . . a poor, bare, forked animal."

In the vision from the cliff, Edgar recreates in substantial terms the journey that has reduced Gloucester and his fellows from a condition of prosperity and importance, through a series of reductions, to a condition in which the individual life is no more important or meaningful than one of the infinity of pebbles rolled backward and forward by the waves. In his supposed plunge from the cliff, Gloucester reenacts his own downward movement in the play, precipitated by his own act in begetting Edmund out of wedlock, which has brought him from being the great Duke of Gloucester to a blind beggar seeking his own death.

The leap into the void is a theatrical allegory for what has actually happened; but what about Gloucester's miraculous survival? It would seem that if Edgar's little miracle play is to be truthful, it would have to allow Gloucester to be dashed into nothing—the word that rings so ominously throughout the play. But is there not something miraculous in what has happened to Gloucester and Lear? That they have survived at all is something, but they have achieved even more, for as one lost his sight he saw for the first time, and the other gained his sanity as he lost his senses. But even beyond these ironies, on the heath in the center of the storm, when it looked as if man could be infinitely reduced to nothing, each of the exiles discovered feelingly—not consciously—a basis for his humanity in a concern for other sufferers, both those present on the heath and those only imagined: "Poor naked wretches, whereso'er you are." Man is, they find under pressure, more than a "worm" or a "forked animal." He is a creature capable of pity, and he therefore has a human essence and cannot be reduced to nothing. The gesture, discovered on the heath, expressing this feeling of shared humanity, "Give me your hand," is picked up and repeated here on the edge of Dover Cliff. Edgar, who has led his blind father by the hand from the heath, repeats the gesture of fellowship on the very edge of the void where he requests his father's hand, lest he fall from this fearsome place. In Gloucester's reply, as he prepares to jump, "Let go my hand," we hear his renunciation of any belief in the possibility of kindness.

The fall from the cliff in Edgar's play ends in miraculous survival and thus dramatizes the truly miraculous salvation found by the wanderers and outcasts on the heath. All their lives are miracles in the sense that, just as they thought their humanity was about to disappear into bestiality and nothingness, they discovered their human reality in a way they had never expected. Edgar's exhortation,

> Look up a-height; the shrill-gorged lark so far
> Cannot be seen or heard: do but look up.
>
> [58–59]

is based not merely on hope but on truth experienced feelingly.

True in the same way is his description of the morality-play devil, eyes like moons, horns twisted and waved, whom Edgar says he saw standing beside Gloucester at the top of the cliff describing life and the world as diminishing to meaningless nothingness. Such a view of things is a fiendish view of life which in different terms has been imposed on man by the villains of the play: Edmund, Cornwall, Goneril, and Regan. The morality-play devil is a dramatic image of what Cornwall "told" Gloucester life is when he tore out his eyes, or what Edmund told him when he betrayed him to the torturer.

It has often been noted that Gloucester is a man of the senses, Lear a man of the mind, and that they suffer appropriately by the loss of sight in the first case, the loss of mind in the second. Their regenerative experiences in act 4 follow the same pattern. Since Gloucester is not a thinker, it is necessary that his remarkable survival be translated for him into the solid terms of the morality play. But Lear experiences both his loss and his recuperation in less obvious forms. Where Gloucester is "shown" the diminution of life he has endured in terms of an allegorical perspective from the cliff, Lear faces his loss unflinchingly in terms of the real world. All of society is, he now sees in his madness, corrupt: the great lady is as lustful as the gilded fly, the gods inherit but to a woman's waist, the justice is but a thief dressed in robes of office, the beadle longs for the whore he whips, and the "usurer hangs the cozener."

> Through tattered clothes small vices do appear;
> Robes and furred gowns hide all. Plate sin with gold,
> And the strong lance of justice hurtless breaks;
> Arm it in rags, a pygmy's straw does pierce it.
>
> [4.6.164–67]

This view of all life as bestiality masked by clothes and money, revealed in his agony to the old king, presents in social terms the same perspective on life as that looking downward from the cliff. Again the matter of hands comes up: when Gloucester asks the mad Lear to allow him to kiss his hand, Lear, too, rejects the saving clasp of fellowship ("Let me wipe it first; it smells of mortality") and runs wild in the fields like a hunted animal—his version of Gloucester's suicidal leap.

Lear's regeneration, his miracle, also manifests the meaning of his as yet unrecognized salvation on the heath. But where Gloucester's survival was staged for him in the form of a crude play with the illusion of a miraculously harmless fall from the cliff, Lear's regeneration is arranged by Cordelia with a more subtle emblematic play involving

126

sleep, a change of garments, music, and the forgiveness of a lost daughter, the principal symbols of renewal in Shakespeare's late romances. Each of these symbols expresses some healing power which Lear has already experienced, without knowing, on the heath; and Cordelia, as her name suggests, is the personification of that ability to care for the suffering of others which all the members of that band of ragged outcasts found in themselves in the storm and, in finding, found the basis of their humanity. When Cordelia bends to kiss Lear and says:

> O my dear father, restoration hang
> Thy medicine on my lips, and let this kiss
> Repair those violent harms that my two sisters
> Have in thy reverence made.
>
> [4.7.26–29]

the gesture and the sentiments are a pure distillaion of all those feelings of compassion which found such rough and abbreviated expression in the night on the heath. But for all its grace and subtlety, Cordelia's miracle play still has the configurations of an old-style play in which "Cordelia seems [to Lear] 'a soul in bliss,' his madness the infernal or purgatorial punishment of 'a wheel of fire,' and his recovery nothing less than a resurrection wrought by this 'spirit' to whom he now kneels and prays for benediction."[8]

Act 4 of *King Lear* is built around these two parallel scenes of regeneration. In both a child arranges for his despairing father to feel once again, by means of morality plays, that man is finally something more than a worm or a poor, bare, forked animal and, because he is so, that life is worth living, sanity is bearable. In both cases this new faith is not merely imposed on men too broken and exhausted to resist it, but is rather a demonstration, an extension into

---

8. *Shakespearean Representation*, p. 102. At this point Felperin supplies additional evidence for the relation of the details of "Cordelia's play" to the morality tradition.

dramatic form, of a saving reality which Lear and Gloucester have already discovered feelingly at the very point when their humanity seemed to be disintegrating into nothingness.

In *Lear* Shakespeare makes his peace at long last with the morality play. Edgar's play is crude in its methods and awkward in performance, but it is noble in purpose, trying to restore hope to a man in despair, and it tells profound truths about the world, even though it does so in simplistic terms. Cordelia's emblematic play, designed for the same purpose, though more powerfully evocative, is equally noble. But attractive and true as they may be, they are not finally in *King Lear* adequate realizations of experience. They sum up life too neatly, round it off too perfectly; and so, in act 5, Shakespeare subjects these visions to the savage test of life as individual man truly experiences it: the French army loses the battle, Gloucester dies, Cordelia dies, and Lear dies. True, the wicked die too, in good morality-play fashion, but in the midst of other sorrows, their deaths, as Albany says of Edmund's death, seem "but a trifle here."

Generations of readers have testified to their pained doubt as to how to take this ending. Is it the "promised end" or "image of that horror"? It allows some degree of truth still to the "miracles" staged by Edgar and Cordelia—after all, some basis of humanity was discovered , though too late to change events—but it qualifies such optimism severely. In the end the actual experience of life excapes any summation. It can only be presented in all its mystery and ambiguity in a play like *Lear*, not in a morality play like Edgar's, and the larger play is not so certain as the internal plays are of its ability to figure the absolute meaning of life or to transmit it to the audience.

6

"The Great Globe Itself"
The Public Playhouse
and the Ideal Theater of
The Tempest

The theater building and its arrangement of space are always a part of any performance within that theater. We have almost lost sight of this basic theatrical fact because the theater of modern realism—like the movie theater which developed from it—with its elaborate scenery and its darkened auditorium, obliterates audience and theater, leaving only the play to seem an isolated, unobserved reality. But the public theaters of Renaissance London with their "heaven" and "hell," their many-sided framing structure and internal galleries, their pit and platform stage, were starkly and undisguisedly present during the afternoon performances in the public playhouses. There remains something mysterious about these strange structures, for despite the work of many generations of theater historians, we do not yet know with certainty the precise details or dimensions of these theaters, nor do we know from whence they came. Were they modeled on inn-yards, bull- and bear-baiting arenas, the classical theater described by Vitruvius, pageant wagons, or the open playing spaces of the morality plays?

We are not quite sure, but it seems highly probable that they were, as the most recent and thorough investigator of the question has put it, "the climax of centuries of medieval experiments rather than a new beginning of Renaissance inspiration,"[1] and as such, whatever their exact measurements may have been, they symbolized in their details the values of that older world. Perhaps we cannot be so precise as George Kernodle, who argues that the major elements of the stage represented the chief images of social order in the Elizabethan world: the throne, the altar, and the city gates.[2] But this is surely the right direction, for the Elizabethan public theater was a model in stone and wood of the conservative cosmology of the late Middle Ages and of the Renaissance.

In his "What a piece of work is a man" speech, Hamlet shows us exactly the way in which the most prominent features of the theater represented the major elements of the cosmos:

> this goodly frame, the earth, seems to me a sterile promontory; this most excellent canopy, the air, look you, this brave o'erhanging firmament, this majestical roof fretted with golden fire: why, it appeareth nothing to me but a foul and pestilent congregation of vapors. What a piece of work is a man, how noble in reason, how infinite in faculties, in form and moving how express and admirable, in action how like an angel, in apprehension how like a god; the beauty of the world, the paragon of animals . . . . [2.2.306–15]

As Hamlet speaks these words, his finger travels from one part of the theater to the other, forcing our eyes to follow, "look you." The outer wall of the theater, "this

1. Glynne Wickham, *Early English Stages, 1300–1660* (New York: Columbia University Press, 1959–72), vol. 2, pt. 1, p. 3.
2. "The Open Stage: Elizabethan or Existentialist?" *Shakespeare Survey* 12 (1959): 3.

goodly frame" is "the earth," which seems to Hamlet no larger than the smaller world, the "sterile promontory" of the platform stage projecting from the back wall into the pit. He moves next to the "shadow," or "heavens" overhead, "this most excellent canopy, the air," and details the beauty of the constellations brightly painted on the underside of the cover which extended out over the stage. Then he returns to the stage itself, pointing to the richly costumed, graceful actors standing beside him representing mankind, "What a piece of work is a man," using terms—"form," "moving," and "action"—associated with the actor's art. Below him, unmentioned in the speech, is the hell, or "cellarage," from which he has already, perhaps, had a visitor, and into which, by means of a "trap," a quick passage was always available in the Elizabethan theater. The name of the theater in which Hamlet first spoke these lines was the Globe, and it was a *mappa mundi*, which constantly, though silently, said that the brave sound of the human voice, the colorful costumes, and the activity which dominated the stage and claimed the theater for man during a performance ultimately took place within a more enduring reality, a fixed frame of earth and heaven and hell, which was not made by the players and which existed before and after the brief moments in which the stage was filled with movement, color, and words.

Looming up out of the London landscape, as it looms up out of history, the public playhouse gathered into itself and gave concrete form in its bricks and timbers to all the many realities within which the Elizabethan playwright had to practice his art. In its stage and auditorium, its actors and audiences, its theatrical conventions and dramatic traditions, it was literally the theatrical and social reality within which the playwright had to work and to which he had to adjust his plays. In its symbolic aspect as an image of a conservative world view, it represented that fixed cosmic and metaphysical reality within which the poet's imagination had to create and maintain his fictional worlds.

Shakespeare did not, as Marlowe and Jonson did,

openly scorn this theater in which he worked, but his relationship with it seems to have always been filled with tension. If we draw back some distance from the various internal plays we have already examined, forgetting for a moment the many ironies which so complicate their meaning, it becomes apparent that Shakespeare never created an image of a totally satisfactory theatrical performance. Something is always deficient in the acting, the production, the audience response, or the relationship of the internal play to the larger "reality" of the play in which it is embedded. The "bending author's" uneasiness about his theater emerges openly at times, as in *Henry V* where the Chorus laments that the playwright must "force a play" on an "unworthy scaffold" and "disgrace With four or five most vile and ragged foils. . . . The name of Agincourt" (*Chorus*, 4.49–52), depending on the audience to use "imaginary forces" to piece out the deficiencies of the stage, "Minding true things by what their mock'ries be."

Dissatisfaction with the theater is much more intense in the lines from *Hamlet* quoted above, where the translation of Hamlet's Renaissance vision of the greatness of man and the beauty of his world into their theatrical equivalent of a "sterile promontory" clearly represents the debasement of a noble ideal of reality to a shabby pretense. Shakespeare's own doubts about the stage seem to have intensified about the time of *Hamlet*, for "shortly after the turn of the century . . . ," as Anne Righter says, "the theater and even the idea of imitation inexplicably went dark for Shakespeare, and the actor, all his splendour gone, became a symbol of disorder, of futility, and pride."[3] In *Macbeth* the ultimate emptiness of life takes shape as a theater and a bombastic actor:

> Life's but a walking shadow, a poor player
> That struts and frets his hour upon the stage
> And then is heard no more.

[5.5.24–26]

3. *Shakespeare and the Idea of the Play*, pp. 155–56.

The boy actor who played Cleopatra discredits his own ability and that of his crude and sensational theater, nominally Roman but Jacobean in detail, to present truly the complex love which Shakespeare's poetry had created:

> The quick comedians
> Extemporally will stage us, and present
> Our Alexandrian revels: Antony
> Shall be brought drunken forth, and I shall see
> Some squeaking Cleopatra boy my greatness
> I' th' posture of a whore.

[5.2.216–21]

Scholars have tended for some time now to idealize the Elizabethan public theater, calling attention to contemporary descriptions of its size and richness of appointments, and to make of it a truly popular theater which grew out of a long tradition of playing and expressed the values of the entire nation, rich and poor alike.[4] That it was a most remarkable national theater with a rich tradition which fostered great drama there can now be little question. But the evidence of the plays still continues to suggest that the playwrights were never as satisfied with their theater as recent critics have been. The desire of the Chorus in *Henry V* for "A kingdom for a stage, princes to act, / And monarchs to behold the swelling scene" (*Prologue*, 3–4) gives some sense of the "idea of a theater" for which their imperial imaginations longed.

This pure theater of the imagination, free of all the limitations the actual theater imposed, existed only within the plays in a type of scene where the imagination of the characters found a free space in which to project the images

---

4. This idealization of the public theater is at the center of earlier works like Francis Fergusson, *The Idea of a Theater*, and Alfred Harbage's work on *Shakespeare's Audience* and *Shakespeare and the Rival Traditions*. More recently it has been put forward in more historical terms by Glynne Wickham, *Shakespeare's Dramatic Heritage* and Robert Weinmann, *Shakespeare and the Popular Tradition in the Theater*.

of desire. The archetype of this scene is the magical circle from which Doctor Faustus calls his devils, and outside which he cannot venture in safety. The circle is the circle of necromancy, an idealized image of the "wooden O," from whence, with seeming safety, the magician-playwright could invoke all the powers of the universe, devils and angels, and force all desired things to hold their visible shape for the two hours' traffic of the stage.

This magical enclosure, this idealized theater, takes many forms. It is the counting-house of the *The Jew of Malta* into which all the riches of the world flow and where Barabas lays his Machiavellian schemes to control all Malta. It is the great curtained bed in *Volpone*, with its hangings that are opened and closed at appropriate times, within which the master pretender acts out his part of sickness and controls all of Venice. It is the walled Capulet garden, in the darkness under the symbol of imagination, the moon, where the lovers, Romeo and Juliet, create an imaginary ideal world of love which is the exact opposite of the hot, hatred-filled, real daylight city of Verona that lies just beyond the garden walls. In smaller form it is the round of Antony's arms enclosing Cleopatra and creating a new reality which the world denies: "Let Rome in Tiber melt, and the wide arch / Of the ranged empire fall! Here is my space . . ." (1.1.33–34). In its most concentrated form, the theater of pure imagination is within man himself, inside the eyes of Tamburlaine, "Whose fiery circles bear encompassed / A heaven of heavenly bodies in their spheres" (2.1.15–16), and inside the minds of great, idealistic heroes of the drama who, like their authors, can imagine a world grander than anything to be found inside or outside the framing walls of the theater.

These intense interior theaters of the imagination usually end in this drama by shattering against the prior reality of the world represented in the theater by the heaven and hell, the space of public life on the platform stage, and the surrounding, containing frame, with only a brief glimpse of open sky above. The hell-mouth, not the magical circle; the tomb of the Capulets, not the moonlit garden; the poverty of most lives, not Sir Epicure Mammon's dream of a world made of gold. Imagination usually falters and fails in this drama, as if the playwrights themselves could not finally believe in the power of theatrical make-believe to transform the world for more than an instant. These failures of imagination within the plays parallel and explain the inability of the various plays-within-the-plays to transcend the realities of the theater and of the world in Theseus's palace, the Boarshead Tavern, and Claudius's court—and by extension in the palace of Whitehall or the Globe Theater.

If the full potential of the playwright's art were to be realized, however, it would have to be in some pure theater of the imagination, free of the limitations of real actors, stages, and audiences, and such a theater could only be created within the play itself. Though Oberon's magical wood prefigures such a theater, Shakespeare, as if his imagination could not free itself from the conditions in which he actually worked, regularly presented internal theaters which were deeply entangled in and limited by the circumstances of actual production. Only at the end of his career, in *The Tempest*, did he create an almost ideal theater on a magical island where the playwright's powers were seemingly limitless. Here the most fundamental questions about the power of plays could be dramatized without concern for the ability of the actors, the attention of the audience, or the ability of the theater to create illusory spectacle.

In *The Tempest*, as Robert Egan says, "for the first and last time in the canon, the artist is hero and protagonist, and his principal meditations, decisions, and actions are all couched in terms of his art."[5] Poets do not appear very often and do not play important or noble parts in Shakespearean drama—Cinna the poet in *Ceasar*, who is torn for his bad

5. *Drama Within Drama, Shakespeare's Sense of His Art* (New York: Columbia University Press, 1972), p. 93.

verses and worse political sense, or the sycophantic poet in *Timon*—and the dramatic poet or playwright has appeared heretofore only indirectly in such characters as Oberon, Hamlet, and Edgar. But in the ideal theater of *The Tempest*, the poet-playwright puts off his cloak of invisibility and emerges from behind his productions almost openly in the figure of Prospero. Living on a mysterious ocean island, Prospero is a magician, and like that earlier magician-playwright, Doctor Faustus, his art takes the form of staging illusions: a scene of storm and shipwreck, an allegorical banquet, "living drolleries," a marriage masque, moral tableaus, strange mysterious songs, and emblematic set-pieces.

> Many characters in other plays compare themselves to playwrights and put on shows, but no other character in the drama of this period acts or speaks so much like a playwright as Prospero. The major word associated with him is not "Providence," but "Art" . . . . On a very obvious level, the play, exactly as it stands, is about Prospero and his magical Art, its powers and its limits, and his "Art" is everywhere analogous to, and occasionally identical with, the art of the playwright.
> . . . he does so many things Shakespeare does: he raises a tempest; delivers the necessary exposition; creates a few harmless complications between Ferdinand and Miranda; oversees Caliban and Ariel; renders powerless the villains; humiliates the clowns; presents a wedding masque; and finally speaks epilogues to his own dramatic production and to Shakespeare's.[6]

In Ariel, the spirit of fancy and playfulness, and his "rabble" of "meaner fellows," the playwright at last finds

6. Harriett Hawkins, "Fabulous Counterfeits: Dramatic Construction and Dramatic Perspectives in *The Spanish Tragedy, A Midsummer Night's Dream*, and *The Tempest*," *Shakespeare Studies VI*, ed. J. Leeds Barroll (Vanderbilt University, Center for Shakespeare Studies, 1970), pp. 58–59.

the perfect actors who are bound to serve his will absolutely, execute his commands exactly with lightning swiftness, take any shape desired in an instant, without limits in their Protean ability to transform themselves into any image the artist conceives. What playwright has not dreamed of hearing his actors say,

> All hail, great master! Grave sir, hail! I come
> To answer thy best pleasure; be't to fly,
> To swim, to dive into the fire, to ride
> On the curled clouds. To thy strong bidding task
> Ariel and all his quality.
>
> [1.2.189–93]

"Quality" was, of course, a standard term for the acting profession, as in Hamlet's question about the child actors, "Will they pursue the quality no longer than they can sing?" (2.2.353–54). Some idea of the range and versatility of these spirit actors is suggested by the number of costume changes Ariel makes during the play: "Presumably he makes his first appearance in an attire that suggests his character as 'an ayrie spirit.' At I.ii.316 he is dressed 'like a water-Nymph.' At I.ii.314 he wears a conventional robe of invisibility and probably he remains invisible until III.iii.52, when he enters in the likeness of a harpy, with wings that can be clapped upon a table. . . . He enters in the robe of Ceres at IV.i.75. . . ."[7]

The audience is almost as much within the power of the playwright as the actors are, and the characters in the play who experience the shipwreck and the other illusions which Prospero stages for them are for the most part completely "entranced" by these shows. Tempest, banquet, and even the appearance of the gods seem to them totally real as they experience them, and because the illusions become their

7. Irwin Smith, "Ariel and the Masque in *The Tempest*," *SQ* 21 (1970): n. 215.

reality, are known "feelingly," the audience can be morally transformed by the theater. Alonso can be brought to know and acknowledge his guilt, and Ferdinand can be made to understand his duties as husband and prince. But even as they seem to undergo the intense experiences of shipwreck, isolation, suffering, and despair, they, like all theater audiences, are completely protected from danger, "Not a hair perished. / On their sustaining garments not a blemish, / But fresher than before" (1.2.217–19).

But Shakespeare cannot keep reality out of even this ideal theater, and this best of audiences is far from perfect. The skeptics Antonio and Sebastian remain unchanged and will not accept Prospero's illusions as reality, while the drunken clowns, Stephan and Trinculo, who take the illusions as mere fact without meaning, are equally incapable of being transformed by Prospero's magic. In varying forms, it has been these opposed traits of audiences—on the one hand, the lack of the imagination, required to suspend disbelief in rationalists like Theseus, and, on the other hand, the literal-mindedness of characters like Bottom who are unable to suspend belief—that have prevented Shakespeare's earlier internal plays from achieving their full effect. The depressing effect of the lack of imagination on the fragile illusion of theater is once again enacted when the approach of those literalists, Trinculo, Stephano, and Caliban, the very images of brute reality, dispels the marriage masque, the greatest but most delicate of Prospero's plays.

The playwright who controls the "sterile promontory" of his isolated island stage is a magician, almost limitless in his knowledge and in his ability to manipulate reality. This playwright was made, not born, for his magical arts are the result of his own experiences, his study of books, and his gradual understanding and mastery of his own nature as a man. Years before *The Tempest* begins he was the duke of Milan, but he abandoned his princely duties for deep study of the liberal arts, was deposed by his brother Antonio, and set adrift in a leaky boat with his books and his infant daughter Miranda. After enduring dreadful storms at sea, he was at last washed up on a desert island, formerly ruled by "the foul witch Sycorax," and there found Ariel, the light spirit of fancy, and Caliban, the creature of body and appetites. By continued study of his books and by learning to understand and control Caliban and Ariel, those aspects of his own primary nature, Prospero at last becomes a magician with mastery over the island. The presence in his isolation and exile of his beloved daughter, Miranda, "wonder," also contributes to his knowledge of self and world, and the powers which are consequent on such knowledge.

As the play begins, he uses his art for revenge by staging an illusory tempest which wrecks on the island the ship of his old enemies, his brother Antonio and his confederates, Alonso king of Naples, his son Ferdinand, and his brother Sebastian. Once they are ashore, Prospero separates them, allowing father and son each to think the other dead, and at last brings them, as well as their servants, Trinculo and Stephano, who has ridden ashore to the place of illusion on a cask of wine—drunkenness providing the means to enter the place of imagination—to his cell at the center of the island. Using various pretenses and plays, all performed by Ariel and his fellow spirits, Prospero manages the journeys to the center of the island in a way which forces the travelers to experience deep sorrow, helplessness, lostness, despair, and ultimately, for those who are capable of it, contrition for past sins and renewal.

Though Prospero has all the accoutrements of the magician—secret book, magical staff and cloak—this playwright's magic comes not from any knowledge of cryptic formulae which command spirits or the sale of his soul to the powers of darkness—not from secret gifts or supernatural inspiration—but from study of books, from full exposure to the real terrors of life—betrayal by a brother, helplessness in a great sea tempest (the usual Shakespearean image for the power of nature over human life), isolation, and despair—

and from a deep knowledge and at least partial control over his own nature and powers, as reflected in Ariel and Caliban. With Caliban, particularly with his lust, Prospero is never easy and manages him only by administering stern pain and terror; and even Ariel, though willing and faithful, is not content to serve Prospero forever and longs for freedom from restraint, as if fancy always tried to escape the control of reason. Prospero's magical art is a tension between realism and imagination, and since he acquired his magic only after his acknowledged failure to govern his dukedom properly because of an immoderate desire for knowledge from books, it is also a substitute, however attractive, for the exercise of power in the real world. Its first motive, curiously enough, is revenge against those who have wronged the magician, as if the playwright exercised his art only for the power it gives him to manipulate his audience, and only late in the play does Prospero learn from his own art—literally from the voice of his fancy, Ariel—the necessity for sympathy with his "audience,"

> The rarer action is
> In virtue than in vengeance. They being penitent,
> The sole drift of my purpose doth extend
> Not a frown further.
>
> [5.1.27–30]

But whatever uneasiness *The Tempest* may display about the nature and the motivation of the playwright, Prospero's plays are extraordinarily important in what they have to say and extraordinarily powerful in their effects. Taken as a whole, they bring their audiences to an understanding of a central pattern of human experience, which Prospero has learned in his exile and isolation, and toward which Shakespeare's own plays had been moving over his twenty years in the theater. As Professor Jackson Cope puts it, Prospero becomes "the philosopher-prince who knows that life is a dream, that in dreams begin responsibility, and that his own task is to teach these truths to the other sleepwalkers in the dark cave."[8] These truths find symbolic statement in the song Ariel sings for Ferdinand as he sits despairing by the edge of the sea,

> Full fathom five thy father lies;
>   Of his bones are coral made;
> Those are pearls that were his eyes;
>   Nothing of him that doth fade
> But doth suffer a sea change
> Into something rich and strange.
>
> [1.2.399–404]

Years ago Prospero had undergone the psychic journey represented by the drowning and transformation of the skull in Ariel's song, when he was transformed from an exiled duke to a magician with control over his desert island; and he now uses his art to make the visitors to the island feel in turn what he knows and what Shakespeare's last plays all show: that human life is a journey in which certainty and prosperity inevitably give way to great loss, suffering, and loss of identity, but then, miraculously before the end, find transformation and renewal. Prospero had already experienced most of this pattern, and it is now fulfilled in ways he had not entirely anticipated, as his daughter Miranda and Prince Ferdinand fall in love, and as he himself discovers that "the rarer action is / In virtue than in vengeance." Ferdinand, after thinking his father dead and himself lost forever, finds Miranda and is reunited with his father. Alonso, thinking his son lost to him, despairs and longs for death, but then repents of his old crime against Prospero and

8. *The Theater and the Dream: From Metaphor to Form in Renaissance Drama* (Baltimore: The Johns Hopkins University Press, 1973), pp. 241–42. Professor Cope's book traces the concern about the nature and value of theater, which I have been trying to deal with in relation to the actual conditions of playing, in terms of the intellectual history and certain deep-rooted philosophic interests of the Renaissance.

miraculously finds not only forgiveness but his son and his new daughter.

It is the playwright's art, figured as magic, which achieves these transformations, and its central role in human affairs is stressed at the end of the play when Alonso and his party arrive exhausted and bewildered at Prospero's cell, and he restores them to life and happiness by pulling aside a curtain, like the stage-manager he is, and *"discovers* Ferdinand *and* Miranda *playing at chess."* Play, both as theater and as game, has absorbed and ordered the lives of the young lovers, and this "vision of the island" restores those who see it.

Prospero's greatest play, however, is the earlier "Masque of Juno and Ceres,"[9] which he stages as a present for his daughter and her husband-to-be. Here the theater makes visible the great gods themselves to tell the young lovers of the endless variety, energy, and fruitfulness of the world,

> Earth's increase, foison plenty,
> Barns and garners never empty,
> Vines with clust'ring bunches growing,
> Plants with goodly burden bowing. . . .
>
> [4.1.110–13]

All the oppositions of the world, water and earth, the nymphs of cool spring and the reapers of hot August, are brought together to dance out in stately form a "most majestic vision, and / Harmonious charmingly," blessing the lovers and endowing them with a sense of the ultimate unity and goodness of nature.

9. In his "Masque and Anti-masque in 'The Tempest,'" *Essays and Studies* (1975), pp. 1–14, Glynne Wickham shows that the earlier scene in which the harpies flap their wings and foul the banquet is an anti-masque, on the Jonsonian model, to the masque of Juno and Ceres, and that the two should therefore be taken as a unit. He also argues, most convincingly, that the terms of the masque are keyed very closely to King James and events in his court, where *The Tempest* was performed on November 1, 1611.

The claim for theater made by *The Tempest* could not be more absolute. It is both visionary and moral in the most profound sense, for it recreates the central pattern of existence, which the playwright has come to understand through his own sufferings and exile, and it affects the imaginatively competent spectator in such a way as to allow him to experience and be transformed by the illusion without having to endure being actually drowned and reborn. "So potent art" as this, like the Shakespearean corpus itself, which comes to an end with this play, fully justifies the heroic style in which Prospero now summarizes his, and Shakespeare's, theatrical magic:

> I have bedimmed
> The noontide sun, called forth the mutinous winds,
> And 'twixt the green sea and the azured vault
> Set roaring war; to the dread rattling thunder
> Have I given fire and rifted Jove's stout oak
> With his own bolt; the strong-based promontory
> Have I made shake and by the spurs plucked up
> The pine and cedar; graves at my command
> Have waked their sleepers, oped, and let 'em forth
> By my so potent art.
>
> [5.1.41–50]

It is the most ringing assertion possible, as if the greatest of the English playwrights had at long last found the figure and the voice to express directly his full confidence in the power of art on the magic island of the stage.

But even as the speech is delivered, the magician-playwright, Prospero, like some medieval poet writing his palinode, abjures his "rough magic," breaks and buries his staff, and drowns his book "deeper than did ever plummet sound." The old doubts about the ultimate value of art in relation to life still are not silenced even in the ideal theater of the imagination Shakespeare has created. The great masque is spoken of slightingly as only "some vanity of mine art"; the approach of those "groundlings" Stephano, Trinculo, and Caliban is able to interrupt the performance of the masque, even as reality has always threatened to destroy theatrical illusion in Shakespeare; Antonio and Sebastian are morally incapable of being transformed by theater; and, his play over, Prospero returns to Milan to take up his civil duties. Art can do wondrous things, but life and death are larger and longer than art. When the performance is over, the actors and the play, however remarkable they may have been, simply melt into nothingness:

> Our revels now are ended. These our actors,
> As I foretold you, were all spirits and
> Are melted into air, into thin air. . . .
> [4.1.148–50]

But Prospero goes on to qualify his contempt for the impermanence of his art by reminding his listeners that while reality may seem to take immediate precedence over such "insubstantial pageants," reality is itself, finally, an illusion too; for at some vast remove in time the great world will ultimately disappear, leaving not even a puff of cloud behind to mark the space it once had filled:

> And, like the baseless fabric of this vision,
> The cloud-capped towers, the gorgeous palaces,
> The solemn temples, the great globe itself,
> Yea, all which it inherit, shall dissolve,
> And, like this insubstantial pageant faded,
> Leave not a rack behind. We are such stuff
> As dreams are made on, and our little life
> Is rounded with a sleep.
> [4.1.151–58]

This is the open and full statement of what the Player King had said in *Hamlet*. A play, baseless fabric of a vision though it may be, is finally a true image of human life and the world, not so much because of what it may say, its content, as because of the nature of theatrical performance itself, its momentary illusion of being intensely real, its actors who assume an identity at the beginning of the play only to lose it at the end, the disappearance of the play into nothingness once the performance is ended. It is a paradoxical triumph for art, in which the theater's illusory status, which had troubled Shakespeare for so long, becomes finally the source of the play's ability to mirror reality. Plays are not real, but then neither is the world itself.

But it is in the world that magicians and playrights must finally live, and so at the end of the play, after renouncing his art, Prospero steps out to speak an epilogue in which he asks the audience by their applause to free him from the confinement of his island and return to Milan. It seems inescapable that he is also speaking for the playwright, who was returning from the stage and returning to Stratford, where he would die a few years later without publishing his book.

7

The Playwright as Magician

In ancient and medieval society, the poet did his work
relatively unselfconsciously, and when an image of the poet
or his work appeared within a poem, the effect was most
often to reiterate the subservience of writing to the city, the
church, the palace, or the great house. Aeschylus and
Euripides debate in *The Frogs* to show that plays are of value
only insofar as they serve the state. The Muse inspires
Hesiod, and Vergil leads Dante through Hell, not for the sake
of art but for the sake of morality. Horace and Chaucer
appear in their poems laughing modestly at any pretensions
they or their works might have to high seriousness alongside
the more important business of the world. By the nineteenth
century the situation had changed completely. The fine arts,
including literature, had become the mainstays of such
central cultural values as creativity and beauty, and the
objectifications of that humanistic substitute for the soul, the
transcendental power of imagination. As Sartre has put it,

> Today God is dead, even in the heart of the believer, and
> art becomes an anthropodicy: it makes man believe that
> man created the world; it presents his work to him and
> justifies his having made it.[1]

1. Jean-Paul Sartre, *Saint Genet* (1952), trans. Bernard Frechtman (New
York: Mentor Books, 1964), p. 535.

Carrying such values and responsibilities as these, now art and artists themselves became heroic subjects worthy of full literary treatment. The subject of epic now could be "the growth of a poet's mind"; of drama, "six characters in search of an author"; of the novel, "the portrait of the artist as a young man"; and of lyric poetry, "notes toward a supreme fiction." The artist—poet, novelist, painter, sculptor, musician—now took his place as hero alongside such traditional figures as the soldier, the king, and the lover, and the making of art became as central a literary subject as honor, war, or love.

This kind of artistic self-consciousness first appeared when art itself began to be thought of as a special kind of activity of great importance to the world. Images of art and artists take shape within the art works of the Renaissance in such a way as to express the artists' confidence in the power of their art, and at the same time to raise questions about and explain the nature and purpose of art. In chapter 1 we have already seen two crucial instances of ths kind of artistic self-consciousness in Petrarch's coronation and Castiglione's picture of the courtier poet, but there are many other examples. *The Decameron* relates how a group of young men and women from Florence escape the plague and avoid death by telling each other stories; the Renaissance sonnet sequences take for their theme the difficulties of writing poetry about ideal love and beauty as much as they describe love itself; Petrarch's *Africa* shows the conqueror Scipio accompanied and instructed by the poet Ennius, who is later crowned with laurel as Petrarch was; *Don Quixote* is a romance which centers on the doubtful effects of reading romances and on the relationship of fictions to reality; Ben Jonson's plays portray art as central to social life and persistently explore the harmful effects of the false artist and the wrong kind of art on society and on individuals. Perhaps the most extravagant display of this kind of artistic self-consciousness appears in Bernini's comedy, *Of Two Theaters*, produced in 1637–38, in which the play opens with a prologue behind whom there is another prologue facing in the opposite direction and speaking to a second audience sitting at the back of the stage. A curtain then descends between the two prologues and the play begins. At the conclusion of the play the curtain goes up again, and in the glare of torches the stage audience departs in splendid coaches by the light of the moon.

Renaissance artistic self-consciousness is perfectly objectified and explained in Velasquez's painting *Las Meninas,* done in 1653. The supposed subject is extremely traditional—the king and queen of Spain sitting for the royal portrait. The faces of the king and queen, however, appear only dimly in a small mirror hanging on the wall which forms the background of the painting. The center of the canvas, now vacated by the traditional subject, is filled by a group of spectators—a child, a dwarf, a servant—looking out toward where the king and queen are presumably sitting, and where the viewer is standing. Alongside the internal spectators, slightly off center but dominating the picture, stands the painter, Velasquez himself, at work painting the royal pair, with the large blank backside of his canvas facing us.[2]

Las Meninas objectifies the modern conception that artists and the making of art may be as central to human life as kings and queens and affairs of state, and at the same time reveals the shift in thought which has made such ways of thinking possible. The emphasis in the picture has shifted from being to perceiving, from objectivity to subjectivity, from the thing known to the process of knowing, from the traditional outward social subject matter of kings to the inward psychological subject matter of the private mind structuring the world. As Michel Foucault puts it:

---

2. See Leslie Epstein, "Beyond the Baroque: The Role of the Audience in the Modern Theater," *Tri-Quarterly,* vol. 12 (Spring 1968), for further discussion of this painting and its meaning in relation to the development of the modern conception of art.

Perhaps there exists, in this painting by Velàsquez, the representation as it were, of Classical representation, and the definition of the space it opens up to us. And, indeed, representation undertakes to represent itself here in all its elments, with its images, the eyes to which it is offered, the faces it makes visible, the gestures that call it into being. But there, in the midst of this dispersion which it is simultaneously grouping together and spreading out before us, indicated compellingly from every side, is an essential void: the necessary disappearance of that which is its foundation—of the person it resembles and the person in whose eyes it is only a resemblance. This very subject—which is the same—has been elided. And representation, freed finally from the relation that was impeding it, can offer itself as representation in its pure form.[3]

Shakespeare's *Sonnets* and his various plays-within-the-play, extending from the Sly play to "The Masque of Juno and Ceres," are an extraordinarily interesting part of this Renaissance tradition of artistic self-consciousness, not only because they provide us with the closest view we are ever likely to have of the attitudes toward his art of the greatest writer of the time, but also because they show those views being tested and formed in the actual circumstances in which the new art of the public theater had to be realized. Whatever low opinion society may have held of plays performed in the public theater, it seems clear that Shakespeare conceived of himself as a poet working in the theater, and continued to claim for his art, at least potentially, all the high values that the Renaissance, in the persons of such figures as Petrarch and Sidney, claimed for poetry.

The *Sonnets* justify the dramatic mode by showing its ability to reveal, as the courtly mode cannot, the complex and contradictory nature of human experience. Profound

3. *The Order of Things (Les mots et les choses*, 1966), translator not named (New York: Vintage Books, 1973), p. 16.

moral changes are wrought on the "audiences" by plays in *Taming of the Shrew, Lear,* and *The Tempest,* showing men the errors of their ways and leading them to deeper understandings and reformations of their lives. The truth which lies at the center of a kingdom is made plain in *The Murder of Gonzago;* the human ideal by which reality is to be judged appears in "The Death of Priam"; human suffering and hope are translated into theatrical terms in Edgar's and Cordelia's morality plays in *Lear;* and the farther ranges of reality are made visible in Oberon's wood and on Prospero's magical island. In *Love's Labour's Lost* art, including the art of the theater, has implicitly the power to transcend the limitations of reality and reconcile the conflicting elements in human life. And, finally, in all the plays but particularly in *Hamlet* and *The Tempest,* the theater in its formal aspects is shown to be the basic model of a world as transitory as a stage setting and of lives as variable and brief as an actor's role. It is difficult to reconcile all these views within some single systematic aesthetic, but all point toward a general claim for a play's ability to reveal by means of indirections the reality of the world, ranging from the factual to the metaphysical, and to change human lives by the power with which it presents these truths.

But this noble ideal is never fully realized in Shakespeare's images of his own art, for his internal plays all fail, to a greater or lesser degree, because of problems in production. Actors are "o'erparted," clowns destroy plays for jigs and laughs, tragedians tear passions to tatters, and the terrified player forgets his lines. Stage effects on the "unworthy scaffold" are as crude as a lantern representing moonlight, or four or five ragged foils pretending to be a great battle; as stagey as Gloucester's short tumble off a step supposed to be Dover Cliff; or as vulgar as a drunken Antony reeling about a bare stage representing an Alexandrian palace. Audiences are as literal-minded as Theseus and the young lovers in *A Dream,* as cruel as the Prince of Navarre and his companions, as stupid as Sly, as talkative and critical as a young lord like Hamlet sitting on the stage, as uncomprehending as Gertrude, or as unchanged by the play as Claudius or Sebastian.

The circumstances of staging a play in the Elizabethan public theater obviously forced Shakespeare to at least consider somewhat pessimistic conclusions about the actual effectiveness of his plays, and other, less immediately obvious, conditions of theatrical production raised more profound questions about the status of a playwright's art. The transitory nature of a play in performance allowed the playwright to see the impermanence of his art and the contingency of any statements it might make about the world. A poet writing for a patron and a small aristocratic audience might be able to believe and boast that "Not marble, nor the gilded monuments / Of princes shall outlive this powr'ful rhyme," but a playwright working in the public theater could literally see that his play was a momentary illusion of a most fragile kind which held the stage for only a brief two hours. When the performance was over the play vanished, leaving the bare theater and the containing world it symbolized as stark reminders that plays exist only within a larger and more permanent reality: "Our revels now are ended. These our actors,. . .were all spirits and / Are melted into air, into thin air." Prospero's recognition of the transitoriness of plays like his masque summarizes what the many other truncated and brief internal plays tell us about their momentary existence within a larger reality outside themselves: the play activity in *Love's Labour's Lost*, which yields to the news of the death of the king and the songs of the cuckoo and the owl; *The Murder of Gonzago*, which is only one of the many other plays in Elsinore; the happy endings of Edgar's and Cordelia's morality plays of suffering and redemption, which are absorbed in the endless suffering and mystery of *Lear;* and Prospero's magical arts, which have to be renounced for the return to the real world of Milan.

Since play succeeds play in a repertory theater, and each play holds a different mirror up to nature, an intelligent and inquisitive playwright like Shakespeare could not avoid some senstitivity about the absoluteness of any truth his imagination might perceive and his plays might body forth. "And that's true too," says Gloucester on being told still another profound but contingent truth about the nature of the world, and Shakespeare's internal plays reflect an awareness of the relativity of any statement a play makes about reality. Plays may lie and distort as well as tell the truth in *Hamlet*, where different plays follow one another with the same rapidity as in the public theater, and even the best of plays, like "The Death of Priam," is ambiguous in its meaning. They may be only the figments of the poet's idealizing imagaination, as Theseus argues in *A Midsummer Night's Dream*, or the pious desire to give the world some acceptable human meaning, as in Edgar's morality play. They may be cunning deceits for practical political purposes like Prince Hal's pretense of being a wastrel, or for evil purposes like Richard III's appearance aloft between two churchmen. They may be variously interpreted by different auditors, as in the scene in which Troilus and others watch Cressida playing with Diomedes. Or they may be only the baseless fabric of a vision which vanishes into thin air when looked on with the eyes of disbelief.

Philip Edwards comments that "in Shakespeare's plays, most of the remarks about the nature of poetry are uncomplimentary,"[4] and it is equally true that most of his images of and references to the theater reflect grave doubts about the nature and effectiveness of an art that depends for its existence on the public stage. But this skepticism should be seen, as I hope I have been able to show, against the background of a commitment to and profound belief in the potential power of theatrical art, which is expressed indirectly more often than directly. Shakespeare was, the evidence suggests, suspended between a vision of his art as noble as the highest Renaissance views on the subject, and questions

4. *The Confines of Art*, p. 2.

about that art as it had to be practiced in the actual conditions of playing in the public theater.

We can see this tension reflected in the characteristic configuration of Shakespeare's images of the theater if we take a step backward and view them from a distance that allows us to see them all simultaneously. In almost every case, there is an opposition between hostile aristocratic spectators and variously inept, awkward, lower-class players, who are usually putting on a type of old-fashioned play associated with the popular theater. The pattern appears most distinctly in *Love's Labour's Lost* where the king of Navarre and his companions jeer at the Worthies, and in *Midsummer Night's Dream* where Theseus and his court laugh unmercifully at the artisans performing *Pyramus and Thisbe*. It is most fully elaborated in *Hamlet*, where the prince not only mocks the professional company performing the old-style tragedy of *The Murder of Gonzago* but provides as well the Sidnean neoclassical theory of theater, with its scorn of clowns and rant, which underlies an aristocratic disdain of popular theater.

Although the pattern is most obvious in these plays, it is still present at least in skeletal form in the *Sonnets*, where the lower- or middle-class Poet's involvement in the theater and with the Dark Lady stands in uneasy relationship to the aristocratic world of patronage and courtly poetry, and to the young noble whom the poems set out to praise. In *The Taming of the Shrew*, the noble lord who arranges the play may not scorn the players, but he does regard the audience, the drunken, muddy, and gullible Sly, with amusement and disdain. Even in brief references to theater in the plays we find this same configuration. The queen of Egypt regards being staged by the "quick comedians" with the same horror as being led in triumph by Caesar through Rome; and Prince Hal is not at all amused by the efforts of Falstaff to play a regal part "in King Cambyses' vein"—"Dost thou speak like a king?" Even in *The Tempest*, where the playwright is a duke, the aristocratic distaste for theater shows through in references to the actors as "rabble," and to plays as "vanity," "rough magic," and transitory nothing. And in the end, the duke abjures his art, breaks his staff, drowns his book, and returns to his palace at Milan. Only in *Lear*, where men are battered and reduced to their most fundamental realities, does the strange art of human necessities force nobles like Edgar and Gloucester to use and fully accept the value of an old-fashioned type of miracle or morality play.

I do not think that Shakespeare, in his images of the theater, was reflecting a deep social division between a courtly audience and a popular theater. As we have seen, young men of fashion may have criticized but they regularly attended the theater, and the court on the whole supported and employed the players. Rather, the aristocratic audiences in Shakespeare's plays represent a certain elevated taste and conception of theater, most thoroughly expressed by Hamlet and, to some degree, Theseus, with which Shakespeare himself was deeply concerned. They give voice and form to an aristocratic aesthetic over and against a traditional popular theater whose weaknesses are given equally extreme statement in the form of inept actors, old-fashioned plays, and clumsy performances. These are, of course, the opposites between which a poetic dramatist like Shakespeare had to work, and he apparently had strong attachments both to aristocratic ideals of art and the practical realities of the playhouse.

It is a measure of Shakespeare's practical and theoretical commitment to the theater, and the full-scale involvement with the world at every level that it represented, that he did not simply resolve the artistic tension his plays manifest either by scornfully abandoning the public theater as an impossible setting for true art, as Jonson did to some degree, or by forgetting any artistic concerns and cynically providing, as Beaumont and Fletcher did, the entertainment commodity for which the theater of the day seemed most easily suited.

The Playwright as Magician

Shakespeare seems not to have conceived of himself as a romantic artist caught in and betrayed by his medium, but as an artist working in the theatrical medium; and while the theater was the source of severe difficulties, he never treated it as mere nuisance but as the necessary condition of his art and the revelation of genuine and important aesthetic issues. The Dark Lady of the *Sonnets* remains to the end a true image of his own complex view throughout his career of the muse of the theater, at once attractive and repellent, sensuous, changeable, mysterious, morally ambivalent, illicit, exciting, and trivial. But like one of the many great figures who followed in the Dark Lady's entourage, age did not wither nor custom stale her infinite variety, and the poet is hers utterly, until he steps forward and begs his audience for their mercy to release him from the "bare island" of the stage.

The image of the poet in the theater who at last emerges as the magician Prospero reflects the same divided and distinguished attitudes toward the theater as the Dark Lady. Earlier Renaissance images of the poet as a religious and secular savior, or as a courtier in the palace of a great prince, are relatively straightforward in the claims they make for the poet and his social function, as befits artists who are supported by society and express its values. But an exiled duke, practicing an illicit art on an isolated and barren island, expresses the ironic situation of the professional playwright working in the public theater. A magician is at once a mere trickster or sleight-of-hand artist and a philosopher who communicates with and commands spirits who control the universe.

The irony would have been somewhat sharper in Shakespeare's time than in our own, for while, as Keith Thomas's magisterial book, *Religion and the Decline of Magic*, makes clear, there was considerable skepticism about magic, there was also enough belief in it to justify statutes against magical practices and discussions about its efficacy on the part of theologians and kings. Shakespeare was careful, as many studies of *The Tempest* have shown,[5] to associate his magician with the most powerful and intellectually respectable tradition of magic, the Hermetic or Neoplatonic system of white magic, in which the name of Ariel appears as a powerful spirit. Prospero is no village wizard, no Mother Bombie, nor is he a mere "cunning man" like Doctor Subtle, the alchemist and astrologer in Jonson's *Alchemist*— probably played in the same theatrical season as *The Tempest* by Shakespeare's company—who also contrives and manages a large number of theatrical pretenses and illusions, all designed to delude and swindle his audience.[6] Nor does Prospero have to sell his soul as Faustus does in order to lure devils to him in order to acquire the powers of black magic.

Prospero is, rather, the practitioner of a "sacerdotal science," as Curry calls it, with a long and respectable tradition deriving from such philosophers as Iamblichus and Proclus, Ficino and Agrippa, which enabled magicians to deal with spirits by way of command, not by supplication or the barter of souls. Prospero's powers are derived from his deep reading and his experience, and they are exercised partly for revenge but primarily for the beneficent purpose of marrying off his daughter and bringing his enemies to repentance for their earlier crimes. His magic, as Robert West points out, "is not natural magic, or mathematical magic or the magic of fascination, but predominantly spirit magic,"[7] and the spirits he commands are actors. Instead of casting figures, reciting incantations, or uttering spells, he

5. The most thorough and learned treatment of this subject appears in an essay on *The Tempest* by Walter Clyde Curry in his *Shakespeare's Philosophical Patterns* (Baton Rouge: Louisiana State University Press, 1937).

6. The similarities and differences of the two plays and the two magicians are explored in detail by Harry Levin, "Two Magian Comedies: *The Tempest* and *The Alchemist*," in *Shakespeare and the Revolution of the Times* (New York: Oxford University Press, 1976), pp. 210–31.

7. *Shakespeare and the Outer Mystery* (Lexington: University of Kentucky Press, 1968), p. 84.

commands his spirit-actors to sing songs, stage tempests, and perform masques which reveal the mysteries of what West, with appropriate caution, calls "outerness."

Shakespeare is following Marlowe in using the magician to prefigure the playwright, but Marlowe makes of the theater a form of black magic, instrumented by devils over whom the playwright has limited control and to whom he must sell his soul in return for a few shabby and unsatisfactory illusions. It is a measure of Shakespeare's greater confidence in the theater that his playwright-magician, like that earlier magical producer Oberon, commands "spirits of another sort" and uses his power to create majestic visions and to effect moral reformation within the magic cricle he draws where all "stand charmed." Yet the Marlovian irony about the theater is still operative in *The Tempest*, where Prospero refers to his spirit-actors as "rabble," speaks of his leading actor, Ariel, as a "malignant thing," calls his great masque only "some vanity of mine art," and in the end, like Faustus, repents, drowns his book, and buries his staff in order to go, not to hell, but back to Milan.

Prospero's spirit magic, while not criminal, was still an unlawful art, and so designated in the statutes; and it was generally understood to be ultimately limited as well:

> No magician, however "white," however masterful, could be supposed to rule in the hierarchy of being all the way to its top. At some stage he had to supplicate, and unless he was a "holy magician" like the Apostles, this supplicati᠎ᔕᴙ⅄ as directed well short of Christian Godhead.[8]

So short, in fact, in the theater, that in Prospero's epilogue the supplication is directed to the audience, on whose mercy and indulgence the playwright-magician, wanting "Spirits to enforce, art to enchant," is entirely dependent for his release from the "bare island" of the stage.

8. *Ibid.*, p. 86.

The power to command spirits and complete dependence on the indulgence of an audience, the "potent art" which can open graves and yet is no more than a mere "vanity," the creation of harmonious visions of the gods themselves and a mere desire to please—these are the contradictions which Shakespeare's image of the playwright-magician holds in tension. In the end the theater seems to have been paradoxical for him: at one and the same time, only a transitory illusion and an image of transcendent reality, a trick and a vision, mere entertainment and a means of directing life to meaningful ends.

The paradox, represented by the image of the poet as magician, of art as mere illusion and high vision, was forced upon Shakespeare by an irresolvable conflict between his Renaissance conception of poetry as a superior kind of truth and his material situation as a professional playwright working in the public theater where plays were only transitory shows. Every aspect of that theater, from his own professional status as a provider of entertainment for pay to the structure of the playhouse itself, reminded him of the contingency of his own art within a reality more problematic and more durable than itself. He might outflank it, as he does in *Hamlet* and *The Tempest*, by showing the theater latent in all life prior to any of its forms or rationalizations, but the very plays which reveal the "Myth of the Cosmic Drama" are subject to the reality of the theater and the world and depend for their effects on actors like Bottom, audiences like Claudius and his court, and a few properties like a cushion for a crown and a jointstool for a throne. In the end, even Prospero must turn to this audience and petition them to free him to return to the real world of Milan (or Stratford). "The best in this kind are but shadows; and the worst are no worse, if imagination amend them," but the playwright, master magician though he may be, cannot finally command but must supplicate the world for that imaginative response on which his art depends.

While the particular conditions of the Elizabethan and Jacobean theater were unique to that particular time and place, they anticipate and define the circumstances in which the many subsequent writers who earned their livings as professionals writing for the public have had to work. The Elizabethan playwrights were the first modern writers for whom the circumstances of a public art dependent in various ways on complex forces outside itself made the status of the poet problematic and the relationship of his fictions to reality questionable. Since Shakespeare, many different images of the poet have appeared which have attempted to resolve the art-reality conflict inherent in a public art by eliminating one of the terms of the conflict. If Milton and the long line of romantic poets emphasized art and vision over a mundane reality, then the Doctor Johnson, the King of Grub Street created by Samuel Johnson and Boswell, who declared that "he could write the Life of a Broomstick" if necessary, emphasized the involvement of the poet with the marketplace and the given social world.

But the image of the poet as magician, which Shakespeare did not invent but fixed and stabilized, holds in tension both the belief of the poets that their art commands spirits, and the view of a rationalistic and scientific society that art is mere trivial make-believe and an entertainment commodity manufactured for pay. The magician has therefore remained one of the dominant images of the poet in the modern world, appearing in such various displaced, and sometimes debased, forms as Goethe's Faust, Melville's confidence man, Joyce's fabulous artificer, Yeat's Irish bards and Byzantine craftsmen, Wilde's liar, Kafka's sideshow freak, Mann's magicians, Borges's contrivers of labyrinths, and Hesse's child who felt that "everything was full of reality and everything was full of magic, the two grew confidently side by side, both of them belonged to me."[9]

---

9. Hermann Hesse, "Childhood of the Magician," in *Autobiographical Writings*, ed. Theodore Ziolkowski, trans. Denver Lindley (New York: Farrar, Straus and Giroux, 1972), p. 7.

Index

Actors, 21; control of theater, 56; Burbage, 57; organization, 57; playing styles, 57–58; Kemp, 57–58; Shakespeare, 58; in *Shrew*, 66–68; in *Love's Labour's Lost*, 70–73; Bottom, 75–76; Theseus and court as actors, 77–78; Falstaff, 82–83; Hal, 83; professional company in *Hamlet*, 95; man defined as, by Player King, 100; Richard III, 117; in *Troilus*, 118–19; Ariel as ideal, 136–37; bad acting in internal plays summarized, 150

Aeschylus, 146

Aristocracy: role in *Courtier*, 10–12; Sidney, 12–13; poetry related to, in Puttenham, 17; support of Chaucer and Petrarch, 24; Pembrokes, 25; Southampton as patron, 25–26; represented in *Sonnets*, 27–34; decline in Tudor times, 29–30; Johnson rejects Chesterfield, 45; Shakespeare's at- traction to, 47–48; in theater audience, 60, 62; as stage audience, 71, 76, 78; support of players, 86; values supported by drama, 90; challenged, 91; standard audience in Shakespeare's internal plays, 153–54

Art: defined by role of poet, 1, 22; Petrarch's definition, 1–9; courtly definition, 10–12, 32, 46; Sidney's conception, 13–15; important in its own right, 38–40; realism, 46–48; theater a public art, 49–51; playwright's concern for, 52, 79; and reality, 73–74; as imagination, 74, 134; its effects in theater, 80–81; relation to nature, 84; as magic, 138–43; Prospero's summary and renunciation, 143–44; importance in modern world, 146–47; explained by *Las Meninas*, 148–49; paradoxical, 158

Audience: differs from that for courtly

Audience (continued)

poetry, 21, 36, 46–47, 61; composition of, 60–63; size of, 61; Sly as, 67; in *Love's Labour's Lost*, 70–73; in *Dream*, 76–77; responsibility for play's success, 81–82; Mistress Quickly as, 82; Polonius as, 97; Hamlet as poor, 97–98, 99–100; the Danish court as, 98–100; Othello as, 119; Gloucester as, 121–25; in *Lear*, 126–27; idealized in *Tempest*, 137–38; deficiencies in Shakespeare's summarized, 150–51

Beaumont and Fletcher, 19; cynicism about theater, 154
Bentley, G. E., 52, 59
Bernini: *Of Two Theaters*, 147–48
Boccaccio, 10

Castiglione, B.: *The Courtier*, 9–12, 17, 32, 147; *mediocrità*, 11; *sprezzatura*, 11, 32
Censorship of plays, 88, 91
Chaucer, Geoffrey, 146
Clown: in *Sonnets*, 44; Kemp, 57–58; typical actions, 114; effect on plays, 150
Cope, Professor Jackson, 140–41
Court: Robert of Sicily examines Petrarch, 3; Roman Caesars support art, 6–7; at Urbino, 9–10; Sidney's position in, 12–13; Spenser's relation to, 18–19, 30; James's support of Jonson, 19; as literary patrons, 24; rejection of great house for theater, 45; Falstaff and Hal play king, 82–84; connection with English theater, 86–88, 90–91; use of humanist art, 87; in Shakespeare's plays, 93–94; setting for play in *Hamlet*, 94–97; courtly view of drama as defined by Sidney, 104–05; kings as players, 111; throne on stage, 130; Prospero as ruler, 138
Crosse, Henry: *Vertues Commonwealth*, 62

Crutwell, Patrick, 36, 46; puritan mind, 89; conservatism of theater, 90
Curry, W. C., 156

Danby, J. F., 19
Denham, Sir John, 87
Digges, Leonard, 63
Donne, John: attempts to find patron, 17–18, 25; criticized by Jonson, 25; small audience, 61
Don Quixote, 147
Dostoevski, F.: Grand Inquisitor, 122–23

Edwards, Philip, 64, 110, 152
Egan, Robert, 135
Elizabeth I (queen of England): as royal actor, 87; Mary as double plot to, 111
Euripides, 146

Felperin, Howard, 117, 127
Fiedler, Leslie: play-within-the-play, 64; myth of cosmic drama, 101, 158; on Hamlet as Shakespeare, 105
Ford, John, 91
Foucault, Michel, 148–49

Gosson, Stephen: *Playes Confuted*, 60
Greene, Robert: *Groatsworth of Wit*, 51
Greville, Sir Fulke: description of Sidney, 12–13, 16

Harbage, Alfred: on theater audience, 61–62
Hawkins, Harriet, 136
Henslowe, Philip, 56, 58–59
Henze, Richard, 75–76
Hesiod, 146
Hesse, Hermann, 159
Heywood, Thomas: wrote *220* plays, 52
Hill, Christopher: on theater as entertainment industry, 55–56; on guilds, 57
Horace: on profit and pleasure, 68; self-image in poems, 146

Image of poet: defines poetry, 1; in